Gweimui's Hong Kong Story

Christine Cappio

The Commercial Press

To my Mum, Lucien, and Yan

Gweimui's Hong Kong Story

Written by: Christine Cappio
Edited by: Christie Fu
Cover designed by: Oiman Yeung
Illustrations by: Christine Cappio
Published by: The Commercial Press (H.K) Ltd.,
8/F, Eastern Central Plaza, 3 Yiu Hing Road,
Shau Kei Wan, Hong Kong
Distributed by: The SUP Publishing Logistics (H.K.) Ltd.,
16/F, Tsuen Wan Industrial Centre,
220–248 Texaco Road, Tsuen Wan, NT, Hong Kong
Printed by: Elegance Printing and Book Binding Co. Ltd.
Block A, 4th Floor, Hoi Bun Building
6 Wing Yip Street, Kwun Tong, Kowloon, Hong Kong

First Edition, Fifth Printing, Oct. 2024

ISBN 978 962 07 0417 8

Printed in Hong Kong

Contents

Eric Berti	*Preface I*	*v*
Matthew Cheung Kin-chung	*Preface II*	*viii*
Wong Yin-lee	*Preface III*	*x*
Stephen Cheung Yan-leung	*Preface IV*	*xiii*

Preface by Christine .... *xv*

Yan *1*

First trip to Hong Kong *13*

Discovering Hong Kong *25*

- Wanchai *31*
- Central and Tsim-Sha-Tsui *33*
- The Chinese University of Hong Kong *41*

Separation *43*

Return to Hong Kong *47*

Finding a job *51*

Getting married *53*
Our wedding day *58*

Living in Hong Kong *61*
The wet market *61*
Causeway Bay *65*
My first typhoon *68*
First job and commuting *69*
Buses *70*
Taking taxi *71*
Taking the elevator at "Easy Prosperity" *72*

A few differences *73*
What I missed *78*

Lucien's birth *86*
Recovery food *89*
Care and education *91*

Settling down ... *95*
Our first home ... *96*
Other homes and areas ... *102*

Mainland China and Macau – 1986 and after ... *112*
Honeymoon in Shenzhen ... *112*
Xi'an ... *115*
Chengdu ... *119*
Macau ... *123*
Transformation in Mainland China and Macau since 1986 ... *126*

Hiking and day trips ... *129*
Tai O ... *131*
Cheung Chau ... *135*

Integration ... *138*
Jobs and Cantonese ... *138*
Volunteering ... *147*
Friendship ... *152*

Food in Hong Kong ... *154*
Soups ... *156*
Home cooking ... *157*
Yum-cha ... *159*
Dai-pai-dong ... *164*

Hong Kong-style milk tea ... *165*
Crustaceans and live fish ... *167*
Peking duck and roast meat ... *169*

Chinese festivals ... *172*
Lunar New Year ... *172*
Homophones and decoration ... *173*
Spring-cleaning and new garments ... *174*
Flower market ... *175*
Distribution of lai sees ... *176*
Turnip cake and candies ... *177*
Third day and lion dance ... *180*
The Moon Festival ... *180*

Chinese beliefs ... *182*

Hong Kong and China – 30 years ... *185*

Conclusion (without ending) ... *192*

Notes ... *194*

Acknowledgments ... *195*

Preface I

Soon after my arrival in Hong Kong in autumn 2015, I had the chance to meet Christine and Stephen (Yan) Cheung. I was immediately impressed by their friendliness, openness, and radiant francophilia. I should add that while Christine showed a discreet smile, Stephen could burst into a very contagious laughter.

It is therefore with great pleasure that I accepted the kind proposal of Christine to write a short foreword for her book "Gweimui's Hong Kong Story". This book is all the more valuable in the eyes of newcomers like my wife and me as Christine gives many keys to understanding better Hong Kong and its neighbouring city, Macao; and China.

This book relates the story of a double encounter. The first one, very touching, took place in Paris at the beginning of the '80s between Christine, a young art student, just arriving from the French countryside and a Chinese student, Yan. Between them, it was love at first sight. A beautiful painting representing Christine and Yan in front of the Luxembourg Palace in Paris, at the time of their meeting, adorns the family dining room. Our two uprooted youngsters seemed somewhat lost in this Renaissance decor, but we can feel this powerful bond that already unites them. Christine tells with humour these first steps of the young couple in Paris, Nanterre and Hong Kong.

The book also recounts the meeting between the young French lady and Hong Kong, an intimidating city if any fits that description. She discovered the city with caring guides, Yan and his family, including this "Mammy" who immediately adopted her with great love. Christine gives us what we would today call an astonishing report about this amazing world city, through the eyes of a hitherto little travelled young French woman. In 1985, the city had little more than 1,780 registered French (compared with 15,560 nowadays) and was beginning to prepare its return to the bosom of China with an effervescent economy and culture.

Christine Cheung evokes with sensitivity and humour this new world, the populous and colourful markets, the love of good cuisine that France and Hong Kong share, and the passionate games of mah-jong. The young French student did not know yet that Hong Kong would soon become her second home. She endeavoured to learn its Cantonese language, which is so complex, its traditions and customs. Christine opens delicately this "gate of propriety" to Hong Kong which will allow the gweimuis and the gweilos as well to appreciate and respect more its richness and diversity. I wish to thank Christine Cappio for this beautiful book that she has illustrated herself brilliantly, delivering an admirable travelogue of her long journey from Paris to Hong Kong.

Eric Berti
Consul-general of France in Hong Kong and Macao

Preface II

I am a regular visitor of iBakery, a social entreprise employing persons with disabilities operated by Tung Wah Group of Hospitals (TWGHs). The café is located on the ground floor of the Central Government Offices in Admiralty. When I go there, I often see a friendly foreign lady with a beaming smile, getting along well with the staff. I think to myself: It is so clever of TWGHs to recruit a foreigner with brilliant management skills to promote business and integration between the able-bodied and persons with disabilities.

Later I learn that this foreign lady who blends well with the iBakery team is not a highly-paid manager, but an exemplary volunteer who contributes her effort and time to promoting the well-being of the disadvantaged. With immense enthusiasm, this French lady travels every week from her home in Tai Po to Admiralty to offer help at iBakery, including teaching English to the team. This lady of exceptional kindness and compassion is Christine, the wife of Professor Cheung Yan-leung, who is the President of The Education University of Hong

Kong.

Mrs. Cheung strongly believes in and is fully dedicated to fostering cultural integration. She is a shining example of Hong Kong's diversity and cosmopolitanism – a vibrant city where the East meets the West. She also typifies many Hong Kongers who have been committed to volunteering in a quiet way. In 2015, the Social Welfare Department reported a record high of over 1.26 million volunteers, 2,800 participating organisations and 22.4 million hours of volunteer service.

From Mrs. Cheung's portrayal of Hong Kong life, I hope readers would re-discover this unique city – a place filled with kindness and excitement, and a home that they would cherish, protect, and appreciate.

Matthew Cheung Kin-chung
Secretary for Labour and Welfare
Hong Kong Special Administrative Region Government

Preface III

Christine, originating from France, is the wife of Professor Cheung Yan-leung. In 1986, she came to Hong Kong and has been residing here for 30 years since then. Not only can she speak fluent Cantonese and Putonghua, but she has also been learning Chinese writings for many years. She has worked for various organizations, devoted herself to volunteer work, and mingled with people from different walks of life. She made efforts to harmonise with the Chinese city which she calls home.

Though not an old acquaintance of hers, I, when reading her words which are written in a sincere and tender style, feel like her old buddy, one that echoes with her curiosity and enthusiasm about this unfamiliar city. I could imagine how difficult it was for an expatriate woman to blend into the exotic Chinese culture, even with the support from her husband and family members.

As soon as Christine set foot on this city, she had decided not to confine herself to a small social circle. She has worked for a jewellery manufacturer, being the only foreigner in the company. Another interesting thing is that she enjoys hanging around in the wet market, an eyesore for many modern housewives, but for her a wonderland.

Her short stories describe her everyday life with a touch of nostalgia. Daily life is indeed the most practical and thorough way to integrate into the local community. Facing a brand new living style, she keeps an open mind to explore all the novelties that are brought by the cultural differences. She learnt folk customs such as temple worship and postnatal recovery food. With a distinctive perspective, she has discovered unusual facets of the city.

The warmth of her Hong Kong story probably comes from her acute sense as a woman – tender yet powerful like water, slowly seeping through the soil and eventually nurturing the land. For years she has been serving the community through volunteer work. By helping others, she brings hope to the lives of the underprivileged and also happiness to herself, which is her most satisfying reward.

Christine has been living in Hong Kong for almost 30 years, during which the city itself has passed several milestones in its development, including various hurdles and the return of sovereignty to China. Being not only a French expatriate but also a local for 30 years, she observes and feels. She reminds us that there are a lot of fine people and happy things around us in this city.

I am glad to write the preface for her new book. When turning the pages, I feel as if I am listening to the bosom talk of a newly-met old friend. At the end, she mentioned that if the communication network 30 years ago had been as advanced and convenient as it is today, perhaps she would not have felt the cultural differences and that she would not have had the motivation to learn Cantonese and discover the Chinese culture. Looking back, we understand that hardship can sometimes be initiatives in disguise. Let us look forward to Hong Kong moving on to greener pastures.

Wong Yin-lee
Honorary President,
Modern Chinese History Society of Hong Kong
Editorial Committee Member, Hong Kong Writers

Preface IV

I went to Paris to further my study in 1982, an eye opening experience that has changed my life in many ways.

I met Christine in September 1983 when she travelled 500 km from Lyon to Paris for her study. I still remember her standing at the residence door, looking lost with her luggage in tow. We spent our spare time in Chinese restaurants, cooking for our friends, hiking, and exploring Paris. I was a math student, doing my doctorate degree in Statistics. I used to look at numbers and equations and knew nothing about arts. She was an arts student, seeing the world in a different way. The fateful union of a Chinese student and a French student, both new to Paris, began an unusual but exciting venture for the next 30 years. She introduced me to art museums and performances. I introduced her to Chinese cuisine and culture. We had one thing in common, our love for each other.

She first came to Hong Kong in 1985 for a month during her summer holiday, after working every weekend for a year in a butcher shop to pay for her plane ticket. She returned a year later and has been staying in Hong Kong since then. During the last 30 years, she has changed from a gweimui to gweipo, from a person not knowing Cantonese to a fluent Cantonese speaker, and from a French young lady to a Chinese housewife. Though seemingly gradual, these changes carry memorable stories that are both joyful and heart-warming.

We spent a weekend in Shenzhen and ten days in Chengdu and Xi'an after our wedding in 1986. I still remember her plane ticket costed twice as much as mine, simply because she was seen as a foreigner. Nowadays, we pay the same airfare to visit China at least once a year for a charity foundation. She has experienced not only the changes of Hong Kong, but also those of China during the past decades.

I admire her courageous decision to come to Hong Kong at a very young age and her tireless effort to learn the language and culture, eventually making Hong Kong her home. This book is about her experience in Hong Kong and China in the past three decades, one that I hope you can all enjoy.

Stephen Cheung Yan-leung
President, The Education University of Hong Kong

Preface by Christine

When two people are destined to be together the Chinese say it is fate. I had never imagined that one day I would permanently live in Hong Kong – the "fragrant harbour", speaking Cantonese and Mandarin with a detectable French accent, happily eating exotic dishes, comfortably wandering in busy streets.

I was not yet 22 years old when I left my family and my friends in France to join Yan in Hong Kong. I loved him with all my heart. I did not think about what I would be doing or what life I was going to have. I was young and determined, embarking an exciting trip of many unknowns. I gradually discovered the way of life of Hongkongers and their culture. I learnt Chinese cuisine and to appreciate the tastes, beliefs, and habits. Although the biggest hindrance living in Hong Kong has been, and still is, the language, I quickly got used to the life in the "fragrant harbour" and made the life-changing decision: this will be my home, one that I will never regret.

Almost 30 years later, I am no longer a gweimui[1] but a gweipo[2]. I have spent more years in Hong Kong than in

France. Do I feel more like a Hongkonger than French? Even though I might consider myself a local, I will always be seen as a gweipo, chiefly because of the colour of my skin. Being called a gweipo no longer offends me but being treated like one does.

I thank my husband for his unwavering love and continuous support during all the past years. I also owe his family for unconditionally accepting and welcoming me as one of their own. Finally, this book is my tribute to my parents who let me go so far away from them and all my friends in Hong Kong who have showered me with generosity and warmth that I cannot find anywhere else but only here in Hong Kong.

In Hong Kong

Yan

All started at the end of my junior secondary when I chose to pursue a programme in applied arts. I did not want to follow the classic curriculum and take maths, literature, or economics subjects like my fellow students. If my mother had been like the Chinese tiger-mums, she would have definitely pushed me get the baccalaureate diploma and go to university at any cost. Even the career counsellor told me that artists only become famous after their death. However, my parents were open-minded and I was stubborn. So after obtaining a diploma in applied arts in Lyon, I then went to Paris to get a higher diploma in industrial ceramic design.

Paris was at about 500 km from where my parents lived, so I applied for a student's residence at the Nanterre University (Paris X) which accommodates foreign students studying in France and provincial students like me. Nanterre was in the western suburbs of Paris, at about 45 minutes – by train and metro – from the 15th arrondissement where my school was located.

In September 1983, a few days after settling down

in my room at Nanterre, the residence's caretaker introduced me to an Architecture student, Momo, a Cameroonian who then introduced me to his friends. Among them was a young man from Hong Kong who seemed to be interested in me. His name was Yan. After learning that I already had a boyfriend in Lyon, however, he was avoiding me. While feeling attracted to him, I was unsure if I should start dating him. Momo's wise advice was to let things happen naturally. One month later, my relationship with my Lyon boyfriend ended. I started seeing Yan. We quickly fell in love and became inseparable.

The Chinese name of Yan sounded like the French name Yann, the Breton form of John. His given name, composed of two characters, was Yan-leung, meaning benevolent and good-hearted respectively. With a name of "Yan-leung", my new lover could not be bad! Yan showed me how to write his name. These two characters did not have too many strokes and were not difficult to write and remember!

Yan was a slim handsome man, with brown eyes, thick eyebrows, and long black hair. Later I would be the one who trimmed his hair. He was so cute in his blue quilted Mao-style jacket. To be sure, he was not totally perfect. Like many Hong Kong folks, he had myopia, which was recently corrected during his cataract surgery. Back then he was wearing contact lenses and when he woke up he could not see much without his thick framed glasses.

Yan was studying at University of Paris VI. Luckily, he was speaking fluent French albeit with a cute accent, so we could communicate easily. I had studied English since secondary school but like many French I could not speak it well. Yan had followed his older sister's path and, like her, after studying French for two years at university he had applied for a two-year scholarship from the French Government, to further his studies in France. When I met him, it was his second year in Paris. Luckily a few months later he asked the French students' welfare office to extend his scholarship so as to give him more time to complete his thesis. His request for an additional academic year was granted. This was great as we were able to stay one more year together.

About once a month, he invited me to a Chinese restaurant to have dim sum, those delicious bite-sized food served in bamboo steamers. I liked to discover and taste the small dishes arriving all at once on our table. The rice flour rolls which are similar to translucent French crepes and the white barbecue buns at first seemed uncooked, but after tasting them I was astonished: despite their paleness they were really tasty. There were lots of various steamed dumplings that looked very delicate and exquisite. It was fun to try a bit of everything. These were only a preview of what was available in Hong Kong. I liked to tease Yan for being richer than I was. Although he was not as "rich as Croesus", after paying for his monthly rent and transportation pass for Paris' three circular zones, he had more money left in his pocket than I, and could afford to invite his poor French girlfriend to lunch.

To go with the dim sum Yan ordered pu-erh tea, the

same tea he likes to drink every morning, a dark tea that coloured the inside of his teapot pitch-black. The pu-erh had a woody flavour and was different from the flavoured Earl Grey tea I used to drink with my mum. The only Chinese tea I had until that day was the Jasmine tea and each time I felt dizzy after drinking it, because as I learnt later, it was too cool for my body (according to Chinese traditional medicine). Pu-erh tea, however, was good for me and did not make me dizzy. I liked it not too concentrated and was still brown-golden in colour.

During the week we came back to the hall late in the evening. We either had our dinner at the university cafeteria next to the students' residence or we ate in my room. It was convenient and fast to open and reheat a can of sliced pork in Szechuan-style or pork luncheon meat that Yan had bought in Chinatown. Preparing rice was also very easy, thanks to Yan's rice cooker. This was amazingly useful. How come French kitchen which are often well equipped did not have this appliance? But this diet was high in salt and fat and I was putting on weight. Somehow Yan did not seem to be affected by the same diet, thin as ever.

One day we went to visit Yan's eldest sister's friend in Paris, a French woman named Blandine. She had just returned from Hong Kong and brought back a pack of dried Chinese mushrooms. Suddenly Yan decided to cook "braised chicken with black mushrooms" at Blandine's place to impress me by showing me that he could do better than opening and reheating canned food. "Wow, Yan can really cook!"[3] Being the only son and with five sisters he had never cooked before coming to France. Later he would teach me how to cook Chinese food and would occasionally cook on Sundays for me.

On the weekends, we often had lunch with our friends living at the residence. Some of us would be in charge of buying the food and others would cook. Because of the group's size, we would eat in the student's common room. Our meals and conversations were varied, and occasionally we talked politics.

One weekend Yan invited 15 guys who lived at the residence to eat a Chinese hot pot for dinner. He had prepared a broth and had to slice the meat himself as he could not find any pre-packed sliced meat at the

Enjoying Chinese hot pot with friends in hostel

supermarket of La Défense near Nanterre, unlike those commonly sold in Hong Kong. We could not sit all around the table and some of us could not reach the pot, so we stood and moved around the table to get food. This was my first Chinese hot pot and I found it really entertaining. I still remember us walking around the table and using forks to get food out of the pot. To be sure, there were no shrimp or seafood or fresh noodle, but Yan had made it as close as possible to the authentic version that I discovered three years later in Hong Kong. Yan's Chinese hot pot was probably healthier, with lots of vegetables that complemented the meat, than our "fondue Bourguignonne"[4] or "fondue Savoyarde"[5].

Making pancakes for me was another way of Yan to woo me. I remember one Monday morning when Yan rang up at my door with a plate of hot pancakes before I went to class. I had a very tight schedule and every day would leave the residence at 6:45 a.m. We never saw each other at this time as it was far too early for Yan. He used to study during the night when everybody was asleep and was seldom up before lunch. I had returned to the residence the night before as I had spent a short holiday with my family. Yan had a "pancake party" on Sunday with his friends and had kept some pancake batter for my breakfast the following day. I was both surprised and touched to see him at my door so early delivering a hot and yummy plate of freshly cooked pancakes.

One time Yan tried to see how brave I could be. I remember the first time he took me to a Chinese supermarket in the 13th arrondissement's Chinatown and asked me if I would mind having a snake soup. I was afraid of snake (and I still am) and had never considered eating any! He wanted to put me to the test and I wanted to show him that I was adventuresome and brave. So I agreed to the challenge and Yan bought a canned snake soup. Later that evening he reheated the can on his electric stove and we shared it together. But when swallowing the soup I couldn't help but visualise a snake crawling up and down my throat. I can't say that I really enjoyed my first snake soup. On that same day, at the same supermarket, I saw white blocks in a bucket and was happy thinking that Chinese could make cheese too. Yan gently mocked me and explained that these were fresh tofu.

Besides, we visited museums and walked in the Saint-Michel neighbourhood, the Luxembourg Gardens, and

Braving snake soup for the first time in Nanterre

through the Île de la Cité. We also liked to go to the suburbs with our friends. On Sunday we sometimes went for a picnic in the forest of Saint-Germain-en-Laye. During longer weekends we ventured further to the provinces by car. Once one of our friends who graduated the year before drove us in his old 2CV[6] to Moulins, a city in the centre of France, where we spent the weekend at his mum's place. Another time we went to Saint-Gervais-les-Bains in Haute-Savoie (near the Swiss border), and another to Mont Saint-Michel in Normandy and Saint-Malo in Brittany. I recall these outings with great fondness. We had fun and the time passed very quickly.

From the beginning of our relationship I knew Yan would be leaving France after his studies. He had always told me that he would not stay in my country, and if I ever wanted to join him at the end of my studies he would wait for me in Hong Kong. I was curious about Hong Kong but he would seldom say good things about it, and would tell me that it was very crowded and very hot. He mentioned strong storms called typhoons hitting the city during the summer. He also said once that if I ever lived with him I would have a domestic helper because it was common for middle class families to have one. I did not realise what he meant and I must say that I quickly forgot about it.

I would have liked to go on holiday to Hong Kong to see if I could live there with him. Sadly, I could not afford such a trip. While my parents paid my basic daily expenses, I could not ask them to fly me to Hong Kong. They had never travelled so far themselves so I had to find a way to pay for my trip by myself.

In September 1984 at the start of my second academic year, one of my senior classmates asked me if I would be interested in taking over her part-time job. The offer's timing was great! However, she told me that I would need to wake up early because I would be helping a stall-holder at the open market. Most of the French markets operated from 7 a.m. to 1 p.m., once or twice a week. This seemed all right with me. But when she told me that she was selling cow tripe and offal I was momentarily taken aback. I would have preferred selling clothes, toys, plants, vegetables, or even fish but could not be too choosy. I was very happy to have found a way to fund a plane ticket to Hong Kong and I gladly accepted the job offer.

I worked at Mr. and Mrs. Choux's stall at "Porte de Bagnolet" on Saturdays and "Maison Blanche" on Sundays. I really worked hard for my trip to Hong Kong. I sold a lot of kidneys, pork cheeks, oxtails, sweetbreads, tripe, and calf livers. My boss was kind, weekly giving me a flank steak, a noble and tender meat with a delicate flavour, or a slice of pre-cooked "Tripe a la mode de Caen". In winter my fingertips hurt because all the goods were displayed on ice. Even with wool gloves under latex ones my fingers were icy stiff. Luckily the Chinese quilted sleeveless jacket that Yan lent me protected me from the cold.

On Saturday nights we joined the residence parties and I had to leave at around midnight in order to be able to get up early the next day to go to work. Yan would accompany me back to my room and then return to dancing with his buddies. After he had left me, I could still hear Michael Jackson's high-pitched "Cos this is thriller... Killer thriller tonight"[7] or the haunting voice of David Bowie "Oh oh oh oh, little China girl" resonating in my head.

In the morning I had to cross the campus at about 6 a.m. to go to the market and I was quite nervous. Nanterre University was close to a slum and some people would often come into the residence to use our toilets and showers. I prayed not to meet any bad person on my way to the RER[8]. I remember one day when a tall big man was walking directly towards me. I was quite scared and lowered my head, telling myself that I was only a small ant on this huge planet and he could not see me. The man walked past me without even paying attention to me and I breathed a sigh of relief. I had always been irrationally cautious. Strangely, I have never felt unsafe in Hong Kong.

During that school year, we were both busy. Yan had to finish writing his thesis and I worked on weekends. Yan moved from the third floor to the second floor, where I was, so we could be closer to each other.

In early 1985 during the winter school break Yan brought me to London. We took the ferry to cross the English Channel. I had never been to the United Kingdom. We planned to stay at the home of one of Yan's secondary classmates who was studying in London at that time. I remember us crossing the border in Dover. I thought Hong Kong was a British colony and its citizens were British. Yan was holding a British passport but it was more difficult for him to get a visitor visa than for me. Then Yan showed me the words "second-class British citizen" on the first page of his passport. I was shocked by the wording. He later told me that his mother, who was born in China and came to Hong Kong in 1949, had no passport but only a Hong Kong Certificate of Identification.

The other event that marked this holiday was that when we arrived late that day in the suburbs of London, Yan's friend was not at home. He and his Chinese flatmates had all gone back to Hong Kong to celebrate the Lunar New Year with their families. He told us later that he had only received Yan's letter announcing our visit after he had returned to London from Hong Kong. That evening was freezing cold and we only had 20 GBP on us. A kind taxi driver agreed to bring us to the nearest Bed and Breakfast, knowing that we could only afford the minimal amount. Albeit this bad start and very limited funding, our six-day London trip was marked by a wonderful time visiting museums and walking around in London.

After defending his Ph. D. thesis in statistics in May 1985, Yan prepared his return to Hong Kong and emptied his room. He left me a few things he had used during his three-year stay in Paris: a teapot decorated with a weeping willow, a cup with the Chinese character "fu" meaning happiness painted in blue, a large flat plastic plate with a blue and white rice pattern, two bamboo tea boxes, a small TV set, a blue Chinese silk jacket with a removable white cotton band protecting the Mandarin collar, a quilted black silk sleeveless jacket, and last but not least, the small orange rice cooker that "had saved his life", as he liked to say. His precious appliance had been brought back from Hong Kong by Blandine and is now sitting at my parents' home in Lyon and we use it when we are at their place.

Before returning to Hong Kong in 1985, Yan also wanted to travel. He bought an InterRail Pass to visit some European countries with his friends from Hong Kong. Unfortunately I could not go with him as I needed to work during the month of July so that I could save money for my trip to Hong Kong. After his rail trip, Yan went to Lyon to visit my parents. It was the first time my father was meeting Yan. My mother went to Paris to meet him the year before. She was very curious to meet the Chinese boy with whom her daughter was deeply in love and hence the special trip to see her future son-in-law. Yan's visit was to tell my parents his love for their daughter was eternal, and he was determined to wait for her in Hong Kong.

First trip to Hong Kong

By August 1985, I had finally saved enough money to buy a round-trip ticket to Hong Kong. Yan had left France two weeks ago and was already there. This was not only my first visit to Hong Kong but also to Asia. I had no preconceived idea. I had always been fascinated by the Far East. My interest dates back to my kindergarten class when my teacher introduced us to the life of a little Japanese girl. The year I turned six I discovered the customs and festivals of the country of the rising sun. With my classmates we celebrated the boys' festival by displaying colourful paper fish in the school courtyard. I also learned how to use chopsticks but I only got the chance to try these tools in a real setting when I was 10. I remember having kept the chopsticks wrapper bearing the name and logo of the restaurant: the "Imperial Palace" as a souvenir. The Asian diaspora in Vienne, the town next to the village where my parents lived, was small and consisted mainly of Vietnamese, Cambodians, and Laotians. To us, all Asians looked the same.

I was very curious to see Hong Kong with my own

eyes. I remember the photos I looked at in the Million[9] when I was in secondary, the same images that were used to represent Hong Kong: the junks floating in Victoria Harbour lit up by colourful neon lights, the skyscrapers mixed with old buildings, and the bamboo scaffoldings masking half-finished office towers. I also wanted to meet Yan's mother. She knew about me. Her only son had told her about his French girlfriend. She did not mind me being not Chinese. The only request she had made to her son was: not to bring home a black woman. I guess she never met and talked with a black person and was anxious of a dark-skinned foreign looking person. Later, knowing her kindness, even if her son had wanted to marry a black woman I am sure she would not have objected to it.

D-day arrived! On August 5, 1985 I departed from Charles de Gaulle airport. This was my first flight and I travelled with Thai Airways. I had asked for an aisle seat because I thought that I would be scared to look at the view below during take-off. The cabin crew was making announcements in English and I could not understand half of it. When the plane took off, I held tightly the arm rests and stared at the beautiful orchid lying flat on my thighs, a welcome gift from the stewardess. When the aircraft had finally reached its cruising altitude and the flight attendant started distributing the menu and a refreshing jasmine-scented towel, I started to relax. The airplane made a stopover in Bangkok. I was in a hurry to depart again to arrive at my destination and be reunited with Yan. I was a bit tired as I had not slept much. At last the aircraft took off and this time I felt more relaxed. It did not take long to reach Hong Kong and soon my ears started to get clogged and the pilot announced that the descent to Hong Kong was imminent.

I had heard of Kai Tak Airport and its exceptional landing above the buildings of Kowloon City. It was said that passengers could see the residents eating noodles in their home. However, from my aisle seat I could not see anything. At the immigration control I got a visitor visa that gave me the right to stay for three months. Then, I reclaimed my suitcase and headed towards the exit. An automatic door opened in my path and I found myself before a crowd of Asian people standing on both sides of a ramp. Walking slowly down the gentle slope leading to the arrival hall, I kept looking on both sides trying to find my boyfriend. And there he was, standing behind the yellow line, smiling and looking at me. We had not seen each other for two weeks but it seemed like ages. I could not believe that finally I was in Hong Kong!

As soon as I got out of the airport I realised that Hong Kong was very hot! The sudden exit from the air-conditioned room to outside really took me by surprise. The air was humid and stuffy and I felt sticky. Yan's glasses got suddenly fogged up with a fine mist. A pungent smell of dried seafood permeated the air. The city was so aptly named "fragrant harbour". We joined the long waiting line at the taxi stand. Luckily a continuous flow of red Toyota crowns kept coming to pick up clients and we did not wait too long. The taxi took the cross-harbour tunnel and in no time we arrived in Wanchai. I found myself in a jungle of tall buildings. When I raised my head I saw signs in Chinese characters and huge advertisings hung on buildings. I had no idea what these logos and posters were promoting or selling. All these signs were like a loosely woven fabric hung between the two sides of the street.

The letterboxes had no names but only the block, flat, and floor numbers. The postmen needed very good eyes to put mails in the right box! But it was certainly easier than looking at the names. How many people in our building were called Cheung? Cheung is one of the most common surnames in the world!

We got off at the intersection of Hennessy Road and Johnston Road, between Heard Street and Mallory Street. The apartment where Yan's family lived was on the 13th floor. In the entrance hall, Yan's family letterbox was simply marked "288 - 13/F". The pronunciation

Street signs hanging like loosely woven fabric

of 288 in Cantonese sounded like "Easy Prosperity" and I understood later why the building was named like this as many Chinese were superstitious and liked lucky numbers. Similarly the number 13 sounded like "a certain life". During the time when we waited for the lift, about 10 persons came in and stood next to us. Some people were talking to each other and I obviously could not understand what they were saying. As soon as the doors opened, everyone rushed in without paying attention to the person next to them. Quickly the doors shut behind us as someone had pressed on the close door button. I thought that this person was in a hurry to return home, but later I saw that everybody was doing the same. Chinese were so efficient but consequently they had no time for courtesy and gallantry.

When I entered his home, Yan first introduced me to his mum in Cantonese. Of course his mum was not like the French people and did not greet me with a kiss. She only looked at me with a big smile. Afterwards Yan introduced me to his sisters. The meeting was simple: just a "hello" with a head nod. Hongkongers were more reserved compared to French who usually kissed their parents good morning and good night. Since I left France, I noted that it had become common for unrelated people, even between men, to cheek kiss.

Yan was the only boy and had two older sisters and three younger sisters. His father had died six years ago. The two youngest sisters were attending university. They all spoke very good English and his older sister and second youngest sister could also speak French which helped to make me feel at home. I was impressed by this multi-lingual family and determined to become part of it. But Yan's mum spoke neither English nor French. She could not pronounce the "r" in Christine and I became Gei-si-ting. Yan told me to call his mum "Mammy" which was less formal than Mrs. Cheung. She had a full round face, black short permed hair parted on the left, and glasses. She always wore trousers with colourful floral pattern shirts. Later I realised that she liked to dress well and her nails were always painted bright red and would seldom wear a skirt. She was from Shunde District in Guangdong province. She was the seventh child of a family of nine children. She had one older brother, five older sisters, and two younger sisters. Only her brother and youngest sister lived in Hong Kong. Two of her elder sisters lived in Macau. Each family member was called by a name specifying his/her seniority and relationship with the person addressing him/her. Chinese were so precise but so complicated! Would I ever be able to remember all these names? It was much easier in France. I called my mum's three younger sisters and my dad's older sister by the same name: "auntie".

At 7 p.m., I had my first dinner with Yan's family. It was so early but the night was already falling. In summer in some parts of France, it was still daylight at 10 p.m. Unlike in France where the temperature will drop when the sun sets, here the heat remained constant. I recall that we drank a dark soup and the broth and the soup ingredients were served separately. It must have been a pork ribs and lotus root soup. I was not used to having soups in summer, let alone with such a strong taste, but I forced myself to finish my bowl. At that time, I did not imagine that later I would love Hong Kong-style soups. This was my first evening and already many things were different from France.

A few days later Yan brought me to a Cantonese restaurant to have dim sum with his uncle (Kau-fu) and his uncle's wife (Kau-mou). Kau-fu was very proud to show me that he knew a few French words: "thank you", "good morning", and "yes". He was also repeating something else that I could not understand but seemed to amuse him very much. When I finally understood the joke, I laughed too. He meant to say "how are you" but was saying in Cantonese "tonight I beat the tiger" which sounded like "comment allez-vous" in French. After lunch, Kau-fu offered me a ceramic rooster figurine which is the national symbol of my country. I loved this interesting and kind-hearted uncle.

A few more days later we went to visit Yan's paternal grand-parents in Tai Po in the New-Territories. The paternal grand-father is usually called Ye-ye and the paternal grand-mother Ma-ma, but Yan called his grand-father Ah-gung and grand-mother Ah-po, as per the tradition in their village of origin. Ah-gung was 82 years old and his wife one year younger. They were born in Shanghai but their parents on both sides were originally from Zhongshan in Guangdong province. Their five children were all born in Shanghai. Yan's father, the eldest, came alone to Hong Kong in 1949. They joined him with their oldest and youngest daughters in the

1960s. Their two middle daughters had stayed behind in Shanghai and were still living there. The youngest was in Hong Kong and the oldest was no longer in this world.

Ah-po was very short, wore large glasses with red frames, and her white-greyish hair cut just below the ears was parted on the right side. With her pair of trousers and Mandarin collar tunic, she was exactly how I had imagined an elderly Chinese to be like. Ah-gung had very short grey hair and bushy eyebrows. He was wearing a sleeveless shirt, a pair of shorts, and Chinese cloth shoes. They were very happy that their grandson had returned to Hong Kong after his studies, along with a French girlfriend who was joyful and adventuresome. I felt bad that I could not communicate with Yan's family members but I knew that I would learn Cantonese, the dialect of my eventually adopted home, when I came back after my graduation. I had heard that many long-term foreign residents could not speak Cantonese which I could not understand. However, I knew the reason later as learning this language was harder than I had first thought.

After returning from Tai Po to Wanchai, I realised how crowded Wanchai was. The entrance door of "Easy Prosperity" building was always wide open but there was always a security guard monitoring the comings and goings. An electric fan behind his back stirred the moist air around, providing the minimal relief from the punishing summer heat. The guard always looked sleepy, thanks to the monotonous humming of the fan's old motor. There was no watchman in ordinary private buildings in France because it was too costly. There were three lifts: one for the even floors, one for the odd numbers, and a third one serving all floors.

Measuring about 800 square feet, the apartment was relatively spacious by Hong Kong standard. There were four bedrooms: two small ones with one bunk bed in each, and two large bedrooms with a double bed in each. Being the only man in the household, Yan had one of the large bedrooms, vacated by his elder sister upon his return from France.

The kitchen was very small and equipped with the minimum tools: a chopping board, a Chinese cleaver, a wok, and a gas cooker. Comparatively, French home kitchens looked like professional ones equipped with microwave, food processor, an assortment of multi-purpose pans and mixing bowls, and many other utensils! But despite having an amazing "batterie de cuisine", not everyone was an efficient and good cook.

Most of the time, all windows were open. Protected by the locked security grill door, the apartment's entrance door also stayed open to allow fresh air to circulate. All the windows were fitted with iron grills. At first I felt like in a prison but then I got used to the steel protection surrounding me and felt safe. Similarly, with time the air conditioners, these awful big metal boxes fixed on the windows, did not bother me anymore. They were noisy but their nuisance was a small price to pay for the comfort they brought in the hot humid summer afternoons. It was not common in French apartments to have air-conditioning because super-hot days were few and our summers were also relatively dry.

I often saw big cockroaches in the bathroom. They liked damp spots and were looking for crumbs. Although Mammy kept spraying them with drug but new ones arrived every day. It was impossible to get rid of them as the windows and entrance door were kept opened and they could visit the apartment freely. But I was not scared of these small individuals.

There was always some traffic on Hennessy Road in Wanchai. Even though we were living on the 13th floor, we could still hear the "ding-ding" bell of the tram. The windows were facing a gas station and taxis came to fill up their tanks even during the wee hours of the night. The apartment had no window shutter and the curtains were defenceless against the bright neon signs and billboards. Hong Kong was a sleepless city, even though each resident wanted to sleep peacefully.

Every morning Yan went down to Hennessy Road to buy a copy of the English-language newspapers so I could keep abreast of the news and improve my English. He returned with local buns too to eat for our breakfast. We then prepared pu-erh, Yan's favourite tea, to go with them. Of course the local pastry was good, but I did miss a good croissant or a French baguette. At that time we could not find any in the neighbourhood.

After her day's work busy at packing tablets and drugs for a pharmaceutical company, Mammy prepared dinner for her children. She did not want me to help her in the kitchen. She said it was too hot and I did not know how to cook Chinese food, which was true. Once the dinner was ready Mammy quickly set the table. She first covered the table with a few pages of old newspapers, then put a bowl and a pair of chopsticks for each diner. In France in my family, we used an oilcloth tablecloth to cover the table and we put plates, cutlery, glasses, a bottle of water, slices of bread in a basket, the salt and pepper shakers, and of course napkins. After we ended our dinner, Yan's sisters washed the dishes and wrapped up the newspaper and threw it away.

After the meal we sat around the same dining table to play mah-jong. Mammy, Yan's two younger sisters, and I formed a team and what the Cantonese called "the table's four legs". Yan did not like to play mah-jong. He had bad memories of his childhood days when he was asked to be the incompetent replacement – the fourth leg – whenever his mum or dad needed a toilet break. One of his sisters who spoke French explained to me the rules of the game in French. If I was interested in getting a domino that had just been discarded, I had to shout "Pung!" and at the same time catch it and display my set of three identical tiles on the table. Mah-jong is a game to play fast and I had to act fast, but I was only a beginner and could not follow the speed. Mammy who was frequently playing mah-jong with her friends and relatives was certainly bored by my slow learning but she did not show it. Fortunately we did not play money; otherwise I would not have any more money left.

After a few rounds Yan would take me for a walk. We would go from "Easy Prosperity" building to Causeway Bay. Sometimes I went for a walk in the neighbourhood with Yan's sisters. Once in the street, they held my hand as if I were a little kid. It was very touching but awkward. I would have never done this in France for fear of gossips. However, I understood they had the heavy responsibility of taking care of their older brother's French girlfriend who could not understand anything and were afraid of losing me.

When we returned home, the TV was still on and his mum was watching either "Miss Hong Kong", a beauty contest broadcast by TVB, or the TV Jade variety show "Enjoy Yourself Tonight". This programme was very popular and hosted by a fat lady artist with dark rimmed glasses called Fei-fei[10]. There was a lot of singing and laughing and although I could not understand I still watched it.

In the evening Yan's sisters were hanging freshly washed laundry on bamboo poles dangling from the corridor ceiling. They did not want me to tire myself. Yan's family was very protective of and caring towards me. The building residents could also hang their washing on cloth lines set on the landing overlooking an inner courtyard. Although the place was better ventilated, only items without much value were dried in this common area.

Discovering Hong Kong

Despite Hong Kong's high density of population and narrow streets, the city was quite clean but what made me jump was people clearing their throat behind me and spitting on the street. I recalled a government campaign on TV against littering and spitting. Since then this has changed a lot and it is now very rare to see people spitting on the street.

People were dressed more casually than in France. It was summer and a lot of them were wearing shorts and flip-flops. French were more fashion-conscious even when they went to their local bakery to buy bread in the morning; self-conscious of what others might say, they liked to dress well. Working women and men were mostly dressed in black suits. I found out that Hong Kong women were conservative and did not like to expose too much skin. There were mixed couples but at that time Chinese men married with gweipos were not as common as gweilos married to Chinese women.

I had seen photos of bamboo scaffolding in the encyclopaedia, the Million[11], when I was small and it was hard to believe that this old method was still in use in the 80s. I was astonished to see construction workers clambering on poles and erecting scaffolding without any safety belt.

The streets were full of things that were new to me. I could not read the huge colourful neon signs, except the trademarks which were in English characters like those of cigarettes and photographic equipment. The billboards and signs seemed to stretch across the street, looking like tapestries being hung outside the buildings to dry. And at nightfall, these tapestries came to life, lighting up the streets with white, yellow, green, blue, and red neon.

Besides horse racing, public gambling was illegal in Hong Kong. Private mah-jong schools were often well hidden. However, there were a few schools highly visible on Lockhart Road. Behind their closed doors I could hear the fierce players inside. The clinking and slamming of tiles were deafening. I pitied the neighbours especially as these schools were open 24/7. In fact, the "students" of these mah-jong schools were playing for real money.

Chinese pharmacies were particularly getting my attention. The combination of the different smells of plants, roots, and animal parts was quite weird and the appearance of these bizarre products baffling. Yan could name a few of them like deer antlers, ginseng, Cordyceps, and bird's nests but many others were unknown to him. I was asking Yan so many questions and most of the time he could answer them. But instead of appreciating his patience, I could not understand why he could not always provide me with an answer.

Construction workers on scaffolding without safety belt

Des Voeux Road West was lined with shops selling "dried delicacies from the sea and mountains". Large quantities of dried foods – sea cucumbers, scallops, octopus, oysters, abalones, snow fungus, red dates, longans, etc – that I have never seen in France before were exposed in boxes on the sidewalks in front of the shops. Snake skins and fish were left to dry on the ground and on the cemented rooftops of the tram shelters. I was worried about hygiene due to the heavy traffic but Hongkongers seemed unconcerned.

I could not figure out the shops with a huge sign of a bat holding a coin. Their doors were open but a screen was preventing passers-by to peek inside. Yan told me that these were pawn shops. This kind of service, once numerous in France, did not exist anymore and people took their valuables to a specialised public institution to pawn them.

There were huge colourful banners set up on bamboo poles and displayed in front of the Chinese traditional restaurants. These posters skilfully made with colourful papers were announcing forthcoming events such as wedding banquets and birthday celebrations. Measuring 10 feet by 10 feet, the sign publicising the wedding of a loving couple could hardly be missed. I was not sure if I ever wanted my own wedding announcement on a big sign like this.

Buildings were very young compared to the 16th-century old edifices in the old area of Lyon, but were already dilapidated. Why did they age so fast? Was it due to the weather's humidity and temperature or the construction material?

Residential buildings in Hong Kong were often called courts and mansions, and had auspicious names with characters like "fortune", "happy", "brilliant", etc. In France, private housing complexes' and villas' names were often related to the locality or the surrounding vegetation.

I had never seen so many opticians, hardware stores, and jewellery shops on the same street. The traditional Chinese gold jewellery is made of 24K pure gold which had a bright yellow colour. The French 18K gold colour was softer and more discreet. There was a period in the late 80s in Hong Kong when 24K jewellery was fashionable and some companies were selling contemporary and unique designs like the 12 Chinese Zodiac animals. Gold jewellery was usually offered as wedding gifts and some of them were not meant to be worn but bought for their symbolic value. I recall one friend who was offered a necklace representing a pig and her suckling piglets as wedding gift. Pigs represented good luck and prosperity in the Chinese culture. I had always associated pigs with messiness and it was interesting to see how an animal could represent something in one culture but something else in another.

There were more police officers on patrol than in France but their look was less menacing than French police. Was it because of their summer uniform? They were wearing khaki shorts which made them look like youngsters. But with their gun attached to their belt, they were providing a sense of security to everyone in the

Chinese gold jewellery with interesting designs

street. But jewellery stores were guarded by watchmen (at that time most of them Indian men) and I realised that Hong Kong could also be a violent city. But considering the number of armed robberies, these watchmen were not a real deterrent against heavily armed gangsters.

Banks were also protected by guards and had TV screens allowing people in the street to watch the current share prices and the fluctuation of the current days' stock markets. I was amazed to see people of all walks of life packed in front of banks raising their heads and looking at the screens. I had never seen that in France.

Wanchai

The street level of Hennessy Road was lined with shops but some stores, like the supermarket we used to go, were located in the basement of buildings. The products' labels were partly in English and partly in Chinese. Some were only in Chinese. Customers were buying fewer things at one time and the shopping trolleys and packaging at supermarkets were smaller than in France. I recognised the biscuits and the canned food that Yan used to buy in Chinatown in Paris. In the toiletries aisle, I could not find anything I used to buy and was at a loss as to what to choose amongst all these brands. There were many Japanese products, totally unfamiliar to a French woman lost in the maze of numerous narrow aisles.

When we walked on Hennessy Road, we always met the same beggar dressed in dirty rags with terribly tangled hair. Even in the summer heat he still wrapped himself up in newspapers. His legs extended on the sidewalk, seemingly ignoring the world in front of him. Like the other pedestrians I avoided his slouched body while holding my breath. Sitting on the ground in front of the CC Wu Building, he often ate food out of a white polystyrene box brought to him by people living in the neighbourhood. The container was filled with white rice topped with a few slices of roasted pork. This beggar's attitude was quite different from those in France who only wanted money and showed their discontent if we ever tried to give them food.

Before reaching Causeway Bay, behind Wanchai fire station, there was a small outdoor area where a few street sleepers were gathered. Further up under Canal Road Flyover, better known as Goose Neck Bridge, a few old ladies were hitting paper figures with shoes. Yan told me this was called "hit nasty person". The paper figures represented the "nasty person", i.e. the enemy of the clients whom these ladies were paid for to hit. Yan did not want me to stop and look. He did not feel right to watch this old folk custom.

The Wanchai Mass Transit Railway (MTR) station was a 10-minute walk from Yan's home. When I first visited Hong Kong in summer 1985, the Island line had only been in operation for a few months. I was amazed by its modern system and brand-new trains. The stations, concourses and corridors were bright and well-lit. What a difference compared to Paris Metro which was old, not always clean, but often smelly. Even the newest Lyon

Metro, which was only 11 years old, was not that clean.

Central and Tsim-Sha-Tsui

Central and Tsim-Sha-Tsui were two other areas worth a visit, maybe even more touristic than Wanchai. Central, the business and financial district, was characterised by high-rises, brand named shops, and a few buildings from the colonial era.

I was eager to visit the museum of teaware on Cotton Road to see real Yixing clay teapots, the famous and highly prized purple-red clay pots that I had learnt about in my art history class. The exhibits were housed at Flagstaff House, a colonial-style building which was also worth visiting.

Every day throngs of office workers crossed Des Voeux Road Central at lunch time in front of the buildings of Hongkong and Shanghai Bank (HSBC) and its neighbour the Bank of China (BOC). A pair of guardian lion statues facing each other and placed in front of each one of these two edifices provided good feng shui to the banks. The setting position of these figures was extremely important and if they ever need to be moved, the timing had to be determined precisely by a feng shui master. I realised later that not only big corporations wanted to know how to harmonise the space and set their offices but also some individuals had their home inspected once a year. These two banks always competed for being located in a taller building than its neighbour. In 1985, BOC building was taller than HSBC building but later it was dwarfed by a new – the current – HSBC building[12]. Then, in 1991, BOC headquarters moved to Bank of China Tower[13], which was, at that time, the tallest building in Hong Kong.

On the other side was Statue Square with the statue of Sir Thomas Jackson, a chief manager of HSBC in the 1900s, and two water fountain sculptures. The larger piece was like a low wall adorned with rectangular blocks of different sizes and colours. Jets of water were splashing on the long relief sculpture. The second artwork was a bas-relief and water was falling from between each of the four panels representing stylised birds, leaves, and other natural motifs in yellow-earth and brownish colours. I would have liked to know who did these two ceramic artworks but could not find any plaques with the artist's name. Across the street on the east side of Statue Square was the Supreme Court Building which housed, later in the same year, the Legislative Council and hence thereafter was called the Legislative Council Building.

On Sundays nearby Statue Square, hundreds of domestic helpers from the Philippines were gathered on Edinburgh Place, Chater Garden, and in the vicinity of City Hall. They were accommodated by their employers and came to meet their compatriots during the only weekly holiday allotted to them. They were sitting on the ground on newspapers or plastic tablecloths and spent all day between them chatting, eating, singing, dancing, and even having some facial, manicure, or a haircut done by their compatriots. Some were even sitting in the passageway joining Chater Road to the Star Ferry building. Among them were a few Filipino men, who were often employed as chauffeurs in Hong Kong. I recalled what Yan had told me once in Nanterre that if I ever lived with him in Hong Kong I would have a helper. I did not need a helper yet. The salary of a domestic helper in Hong Kong was not high and many families could employ one. I was already aware of the advantage and the good fortune Hong Kong women had, as employing a full-time live-in housekeeper in France was very expensive and, even for the middle class, a luxury.

Yan asked me whether I could differentiate the Filipina from the Chinese women. I replied that they all looked more or less the same to me. They all had black straight hair and black eyes. Yan mocked me and asked me if I could recognise him among the other men. It was also very difficult to guess the age of Asian people as they looked younger than their actual age. Elderly usually dyed their hair (unlike in France) and the few

Filipino maids in Central on Sundays

youngsters who had auburn hair were remarkable. The few ones with blond hair were even more noticeable and looked like the triad members depicted in the movies, with tattoos of dragons and other signs on their forearms and calves as well as flashy 24K gold chains. Later with more exposure to Asian faces I started to differentiate facial features better. Similarly, at that time, I could not distinguish between Tagalog and Cantonese and the two languages were both incomprehensible for me. In French we would have said, "It's Chinese!"

At the exit of the Chater Road underpass was the Star Ferry Pier, where the ferries crossing to Tsim-Sha-Tsui and Hung Hom, on the Kowloon Peninsula, departed. Newsagents were gathered in front of the entrance of the Star Ferry Pier. There was also an English language bookstore and a fast-food called "Maxim's", not to be confused with "Maxim's of Paris"! Next to the Star Ferry Pier was the City Hall where Yan and I would later get married.

In Edinburgh Place old men were pulling rickshaws and trying to get the attention of tourists. They tried to entice me to take a ride in their vehicle. It must have been exotic but I did not feel like a tourist and declined their invitation. On the plaza an old man was selling tuberose buds for a few dollars. I recognised the pleasant scent of the small white flowers that taxi drivers were putting on the dashboard of their vehicle to cover the cigarette smell.

Also in Edinburgh Place many tourists were lining up, waiting for a taxi to bring them to the Peak Tram terminus to take the funicular railway, the quickest way to reach Victoria Peak, and admire the scenic view from there. One of Yan's secondary classmates had driven us to the Peak one evening and I was astonished by the spectacular view. Two years later my sister brought me

Rickshaw in Edinburgh Place

to a panoramic point in Los Angeles but after having seen Hong Kong at night it did not look very special.

The wharfs going to the outlying islands were located further west along the waterfront and Queen's Pier, where the governors had landed and two more would land, was on the other side opposite to City Hall. Private junks also departed from Queen's Pier and I could see groups of people who were waiting to embark. They were probably going to sail to one of the outlying islands to eat seafood or to the east coast of Sai Kung Peninsula to swim at Tai Long Wan. The Star Ferry Pier has been moved further west at the end of 2006 but Queen's Pier

View of Victoria Harbour from the ferry

was demolished in early 2008.

Tsim-Sha-Tsui, on the Kowloon Peninsula, was even more crowded than Central. The double-decker buses of Kowloon Motor Bus were red and beige whereas on Hong Kong Island those of China Motor Bus were blue. The Clock Tower in granite and red brick was the only element left of the old Kowloon railway station. The Hong Kong Museum of Art and the Hong Kong Cultural Centre were not built yet, and the statue of Bruce Lee[14] and the brass star of Jackie Chan did not exist either. Yan showed me the building further up, the Space Museum, where he watched French films regularly during our

separation. Facing the windowless egg-shaped building and across Salisbury Road was the Peninsula Hotel and its fleet of Rolls-Royces. Many tourists were taking pictures in front of the water fountain. We then followed a tourist into the hotel but we came out quickly because we felt out of place. Wow, all these chandeliers: it looked like we were in the Palace of Versailles!

Nathan Road was packed with tourists and lots of Indian vendors kept asking us if we wanted to buy "copy watch", pointing at their wrists. Other traders asked us if we wanted to have a custom-made suit and offered us their business cards. Of course we were not interested and ignored them. It was annoying to be accosted all the time. It was very hot and we popped into the many stores just to have a blast of air-conditioning. We did not stay too long inside as I had forgotten to bring with me a jacket and was afraid to catch a cold. Furthermore, the salespersons were turning their back on me to take care of local clients. Yan comforted me, telling me that they were not afraid of me but were only scared of speaking English. Due to the above observations, my first impression of Tsim-Sha-Tsui was not very good.

What I enjoyed most was the ferry ride back to Central. Sitting on the wooden benches, from the middle of the harbour, the high-rises looked much smaller but also more densely packed than viewed from the street-level. The view was magnificent. Each time a boat or a cargo ship sailed next to us our ferry slowed down or changed direction to avoid them and we were moved from side to side. The trip did not take long, then our ferry bumped into the berth and we were again swung from side to side while the crew members in sailor-style uniform were busy attaching a heavy rope around a wooden pole. No sooner the footbridge was lowered than everyone rushed to cross it to be the first to set foot on the ground. As always people were in a hurry.

The Chinese University of Hong Kong

One day Yan brought me to visit the Chinese University of Hong Kong (CUHK) where he studied from 1978 to 1982. We took a cross-harbour bus, got off at the first stop after the tunnel, and walked to the train station terminus in Hung Hom. Behind the station was the Hong Kong Coliseum, a large multi-purpose room which looked like, from outside, a large rectangular tray.

When Yan was at CUHK he took the train once a week to go home on weekends. At that time, Hong Kong railway used a single-track system with passing loops at each station. There was only one train every hour and each journey typically took him one hour. On that day, however, it only took us only 30 minutes to reach University Station from Hung Hom, due chiefly to the previous year's electrification and conversion to a double-track system which had increased the train frequency and speed.

The campus situated on a hill between Shatin and Tai Po in the New-Territories, enjoyed magnificent views of Tolo Harbour and the surrounding countryside. It was certainly a place conducive to academic pursuit, unlike

Wanchai which was abuzz with activities of various kinds – legitimate or otherwise. That day was a very hot one, and we took a shuttle bus up the hill to the United College. I suddenly recalled a ghost story that two Hong Kong friends we met in Paris were told when they were both at CUHK. It was said that some students had seen a ghost in one of the classrooms. Hiiii!

Yan was very proud of his alma mater and retained fond memories of his student days that had changed his life. He had made a lunch appointment with a French Jesuit Father and a Great China specialist who was a lecturer at the university. He recounted his student life and experience in France to him and that he could not understand what people were talking about during his first month in France, albeit his two years of training in French in Hong Kong. However, he had adjusted fast. I wondered if I could do the same should I decide to permanently reside here in Hong Kong.

Separation

On September 2, 1985, I was again at Kai Tak Airport. This was the end of my vacation in Hong Kong and the beginning of a long separation. We were going to stay apart for 10 months and I felt sad. I had to go back to Paris to finish my third and last academic year. On leaving, Mammy gave me a pair of gold earrings of the same gold colour I had seen in the many jewellery shops on Hennessy Road during my stay. Despite the shiny colour, I wore them as a souvenir of my first visit to Hong Kong and Yan's mum.

I had stayed for one month and had a pretty good idea of what to expect if I had to live there. Yes, Hong Kong was indeed crowded and hot. For sure Yan had not lied to me. Dealing with the weather and a jam-packed environment did not seem too difficult. I knew that I would be back! Strangely at that time I was not thinking of what I would be doing jobwise. I knew Yan and I would be together again in a few months and that we would deal with it then.

During my third and last academic year in Paris, the

electronic mails did not exist. I wrote to Yan once a week, most often aerogrammes. Yan also sent me lots of letters with cute bookmarks inside. During the weekend I was still selling tripe at the Choux's stall.

Selling tripe to earn money to visit Yan in Hong Kong

Yan phoned me once when I was at my parents' place during the Christmas holiday. It was impractical to call me at the residence. There was only one telephone for the 30 students living on my floor. Very often the line was engaged or nobody was free to pick up someone else's call. Furthermore there was also the problem of time difference between France and Hong Kong. When I heard Yan's voice, I was touched and cried. Although I knew I only had to wait for another six months before seeing him, I was still sad.

Once I passed my final exams, I went to say farewell to my parents. They knew I was going to join Yan in Hong Kong but did not know exactly when I would be back. Neither did I. They never objected to my having a Chinese boyfriend and neither did they prevent me from leaving or show their worries. My elder sister had already left home for the USA two years earlier and had not returned yet. My younger brother had left two weeks before to New-Caledonia for his military service. I was their third child to go abroad within such a short span of time. It must have been in our blood to travel and see the world, although at that time we did not know it. 20 years later, at the age of 68, my dad discovered while constructing his family tree that his paternal grandfather, an Italian man, had lived in Algeria and Bulgaria. Travelling from the Piedmont region of Italy to North Africa and South-eastern Europe in the late 19th century must have required more courage than for me flying from Paris to Hong Kong.

For sure I was sad to leave my family but at peace

with myself knowing that my parents trusted me and were happy for me. I told them I would write often and phone them regularly. They would have never imagined that less than two months later their daughter would be married. Neither did I.

Aerogrammes to Yan and plane flying over Kowloon City

Return to Hong Kong

On June 25, 1986 I went to Charles de Gaulle airport and again travelled to Hong Kong via Bangkok.

I will always remember my first two trips to Hong Kong, particularly flying over the densely packed buildings of Kowloon City and the first sensations when I got out of the airport, the smell of dried seafood, the heat, and humidity. After the opening of the new airport on Lantau Island, the arrival to Hong Kong which was magical and exciting had never been the same. Chek Lap Kok was just another airport, far away from the city, but the Kowloon City residents could now sleep peacefully.

After 10 months of separation, we were finally reunited. I had no idea of what I was going to do but was not worried. I loved Yan and that was all that counted. Yan had lived in France for three years and I thought I should try to live in Hong Kong for three years too. Then we could decide in which part of the world we wanted to live.

Since his return to Hong Kong, Yan was working at City Polytechnic (which later became City University).

We decided to live for a few months with Yan's family until I got familiar with the new environment and found a flat for ourselves. I was glad that Mammy did not object to our decision to move on our own. Unlike many Chinese mums, she did not mind. My mum was worried that living with my in-laws would create conflicts. Even in France, the relationship between mother-in-law and daughter-in-law was not easy. In my case, I would also have cultural and communication problems.

Although Yan's friends were working, they were still living together with their parents. At that time I was surprised as French young people were eager to leave the family nest and be independent as soon as they could. Today French are like Hongkongers and remain with their parents as long as possible so as to make savings. But in Hong Kong, the main deterrent for working youngsters to move out of their parents' home was the sky-high rents and young people were only moving after getting married.

The rent of the flat in which Yan's family was living was reasonable comparatively to its size but the building was old and noisy. Yan did not like me taking the lift on my own and was always worried that something might happen to me. He often said that Wanchai was composed of "many-mixed", the Cantonese slang term for all kinds of people.

I had visited a public flat the year before. Yan's grand-parents lived in Tai Yuen Estate, the first set of public housing estate built in Tai Po. Clothes were hung out to dry on bamboo poles and these bits of colour were brightening up the otherwise sad facades. The complex, built in 1980, was relatively new but the corridors, serving more than 40 apartments per floor, were already dark and dirty. The layout reminded me of Nanterre University's residence. To live in this type of flat was fine when I was a student but I would not have liked to live there for the rest of my life. Yan's grand-parents had been allocated a flat in Tai Tak House. Ah-gung and Ah-po's flat was simple. On the right of the living room there were two bedrooms separated by removable partitions. There was no bathroom and the lavatory, located between the bedroom and the kitchen, was equipped with a hose and a shower head. The kitchen was on the loggia and, like that of Yan's family, was equipped with the minimum tools. Public housing in France was no better than that in Hong Kong. The subsidised flats in France were described as "rabbit hutches" – to express their tininess. However, the towers were never as tall and the population density never as high as in Hong Kong.

The best for us would be to live in a private and recently built flat like "City One", a residential complex located in Shatin where one of Yan's friends lived. We had visited his apartment once in 1985. At that time the complex already consisted of more than 30 towers and housed more than 20,000 people. From high above, the complex looked like a jungle of bamboo. A flat of about 400 square-feet would be large enough for the two of us. In addition, it was very convenient with shops and public transportation within reach. I could live in "City One" but I liked Hong Kong Island better. Hong Kong Island had more character and more charm than this new town. Furthermore, I started to get used to Wanchai and we would be closer to Yan's mum. Anyhow we would look for a flat later.

But first of all I needed to find a job to solve my identity card issue. I was permitted to stay in Hong Kong until September 26, 1986. Some people were suggesting me to go to Macau, which was still a Portuguese colony at that time, to get a new three-month visa when re-entering Hong Kong. This process was common but I was also told that I could only use this tactic a few times. Another way to reside legally without hassles and for a longer time was to get a Hong Kong Identity Card. For that, I needed a sponsor thus a person who would support me financially, i.e. a husband or an employer. I was not thinking of getting married so I started to look for a job.

Finding a job

I went first to the Fringe Club which was housed in a beautiful brick and stucco building in Central. Each year the Fringe Club organised art exhibitions and provided pottery classes to adults and children. I went to ask them if they needed a teacher. I could not throw clay bowls on a potter's wheel because I had never learnt that technique, but I could teach other techniques and how to make sculptures. Unfortunately they had enough teachers. I looked for jobs in the ceramic industry but without much success.

What else could I do? I knew French lessons were in high demand. What about teaching French? I was told that the Alliance Française de Hong Kong was employing teachers without degree or prior experience. Yan went with me to meet someone at the Alliance Française de Hong Kong who offered me to teach a few hours per week. Unfortunately this was not enough to sponsor me and I could not work with a tourist visa. But the funny thing was that he was ready to employ Yan because he had an ID card and spoke fluent French. Before leaving, the man suggested that I should marry Yan to solve my problem. His remark surprised me but was not unreasonable. Once at home Yan and I talked about getting married. Sooner or later we would get married, so why not as soon as possible? Of course this was not a marriage of convenience. We knew we loved each other and I knew that he would make me happy. So, we agreed to get married.

3-month residence permit in Hong Kong

Getting married

A few days after my visit to the Alliance Française de Hong Kong, Yan and I went to the marriage registration office in Admiralty. The civil servant asked me whether I was already married or not. I got confused with the question tag and replied "Yes" instead of "No". She gave a bewildered look at Yan and asked him again in Cantonese. Yan quickly told her that I was not married and I also provided the proper answer: "No. I am not married". Then the woman asked us on which date we wanted to get married. We still surprised her when Yan said, "As soon as possible". Chinese liked to choose an auspicious date but we had not consulted anybody and in less than one minute had made up our mind. Our wedding will take place on Monday, July 21 and the ceremony will be held at the City Hall marriage registry in Central. The Cotton Tree Drive branch was not available. The latter was in high demand due to its idyllic setting for wedding pictures. We did not mind at all. Now there was no need to worry about how long I could stay.

The same day we announced to Mammy that we were going to get married. She was delighted and immediately talked about organising a traditional Chinese wedding which, as I discovered later, consisted of mah-jong parties, endless photo sessions, and a banquet. We had no time to prepare any elaborate wedding. Furthermore it would have been too complicated, tiring, and expensive. On that evening Mammy wept gently in her bed. I sat beside her and she took my hand and patted it softly. Yan's sisters explained to me that she was sad because she could not convince her only son. I supported Yan's decision and did not feel necessary to have a traditional ceremony. We did not think that getting married was a one-day celebration to please friends and relatives. Mammy finally relented with much disappointment.

I had to inform my parents. We could not call directly abroad from Yan's place, so we went to the call centre of Cable & Wireless in a brand-new building at Exchange Square in Central. We queued up to pay for the communication in advance and then waited until a cabin was free. There were many people, notably Filipinos who were taking advantage of their day off to call their families. A one-minute call was relatively expensive[15], about 10 HKD per minute. Today, for the same amount I can speak for 20 minutes and even call for free. I finally had my mother on the line and I broke the news to her. She understood that it was important to legalise my stay since it would be easier to find a job but my parents did not have enough time to prepare for a trip and would not come to Hong Kong. Anyhow, we were only getting married at the registry office and maybe we could get married again and have a celebration in France later. Unfortunately for my parents this never happened.

It was difficult to imagine what my parents must have thought. They had never been to Hong Kong and not even Asia. Hong Kong was well-known for its cheap manufactured products, its martial arts legend Bruce Lee, and for being the largest brandy consumer in the world. But another of its facets which was less impressive was drug trafficking. Their daughter was going to settle down in Hong Kong far away from them. Were they anxious of her future life? Would she ever come back and visit them? How often? My parents must have been disappointed for not being able to attend the wedding and witness the first of their three children tying the knot. However, they must have felt that I was happy and knew what I was doing because they did not try to stop me. They did not mind having a Chinese son-in-law. My father must have had an understanding for mixed-cultural marriage in his blood without knowing it. When constructing his family tree, at the age of 68, he found out that his Italian grand-father had married a Hispano-French lady while he was building railways in Algeria, back in 1865. His grand-parents had eight children together and the youngest one, his dad, was born in 1888. Four of their children were born in Algeria, three in Italy and one in Bulgaria. My parents had let me study art and go to Paris. I had met young girls at the university residence who were studying law or medicine, not because they liked the subjects but because their mums wanted them to find a "good" husband among their classmates. I did not meet any future artists but destiny put me on Yan's path. He was certainly not an artist but a pragmatic guy. And he was a gentle person. I had no idea what he would be doing later except that he would not be staying in France. Was I too naive? I trusted him. This was my destiny. I might not have a career in the arts but a life with someone I loved. I would certainly have an interesting life albeit one that I had never imagined.

We went to Heard Street, a small road next to "Easy Prosperity" building, to order invitation cards for my family and friends in France at one of the numerous print shops. We chose a light pink card with a little boy and a little girl kissing each other. Mammy was going to inform her relatives orally and Yan his colleagues. When we got the cards, we saw a typo mistake but as it was not on our names, we did not bother and send the cards just as they were. My parents could not read English – they had never learnt it at school – and in fact nobody paid attention, except my sister!

At that time my brother was doing his military service in New-Caledonia. He had met Yan in July 1985 when Yan went to meet my father and at the same time say goodbye to my family. He later told me he had never drunk so much as on the day when he received our card. My sister was living in Los Angeles and only saw Yan once when she went to visit Paris before going to the United States in May 1984. When she got her mails on that day and saw a pink envelope she wondered what news she was going to find. She could not believe her eyes: "Boy, it's already done!"

We still had to inform Yan's grand-parents. Yan phoned them and they wanted us to visit them in Tai Po. They kept smiling and chatting happily. They were old and would not travel to Hong Kong Island to attend our wedding. All of a sudden Ah-gung got a pair of 24K gold bracelets out of a brown envelope that he had custom-made at the birth of Yan and kept in a safe deposit box until that day. These bracelets had been waiting for me since 1959, when I was not even born! Had Yan's grand-parents ever thought that their only grandson would marry a gweimui? I was grateful that like my parents and Yan's mum, they did not object to our wedding and were welcoming me to the Cheung family.

What were we going to wear? Yan did not want to buy any new clothes for himself. Yan's elder sister proposed to lend me her black cheongsam. I would have never imagined getting married in black, the colour of mourning for us. It had a red and gold floral pattern on the neckline and slit and I bought a pair of red shoes to brighten the outfit. Mammy offered us our wedding rings, in 24K gold as per the tradition, and had our names and our wedding

Gold bracelets from Ah-gung waiting for me since 1959

date engraved inside. She also gave me a black evening pouch with a Chinese floral pattern and a black velvet edge.

I had informed my parents. Yan had finally convinced his Mum and told his grand-parents. We then went to visit Yan's dad at the columbarium in Tsuen Wan where he was resting.

Our wedding day

The wedding day came. I was wearing Yan's elder sister's cheongsam, the gold earrings Mammy had offered me the previous year, and Ah-gung and Ah-po's gold bangles. I had put a bit of makeup and held a mix-coloured bouquet of flowers bought earlier at the market

Wedding day at City Hall

by my sisters-in-law, and Mammy's evening pouch. Yan was wearing a pair of beige trousers and had put our wedding rings in one of the pockets, a striped light shirt, and a tie. He looked so solemn! We were ready and waited anxiously for one of Yan's friends who had agreed to be our chauffeur for this occasion to drive us to the marriage registry.

It was raining and the traffic was dense. We had to be at the City Hall Marriage Registry at 4:30 p.m. We were the last couple to get married on the day and we were 15 minutes late. My Hong Kong girlfriend whom I met in Paris and her husband greeted me and gave me a lovely wedding ring cushion. It was so thoughtful of them! I had not thought of this detail. We rushed into the marriage registry room under the eyes of 40 people who were waiting anxiously for us. Most of them had never seen me and were curious to see what the gweimui looked like.

Mammy was Yan's witness and his eldest sister mine. Mammy was wearing a beautiful light green pinstripe skirt with a matching blouse. This was the first time I saw her not wearing trousers. Once our wedding was registered, we went to City Hall Memorial Garden to take photographs. The black marble wall was certainly a less flamboyant background than the Flagstaff House where my girlfriend (who gave me the wedding rings cushion) took her wedding photos the year before. Our photographer was one of Yan's secondary classmates. After the photos session we all went for a drink at the City Hall coffee shop. Later in the evening we celebrated with a simple dinner with Mammy, three sisters of Yan (two of Yan's sisters were not there: one was studying in France and the other was travelling in China) and three of Yan's classmates, at a restaurant in Wanchai famous for the "Imperial Concubine Chicken", an impressive name for a simple chicken cooked in wine!

When today I think of our wedding day I realised it was simple but stressful. I always thanked Yan for not having a traditional marriage. I carefully put away Yan's grand-parents' bangles and they are patiently waiting for their next owner. I finally took time to look at my wedding ring. Although I found its colour too shiny, it was a symbol of our love. Yan and I wore them for quite a number of years until Yan's fingers got bigger and his ring could no longer fit, so we both stopped wearing them.

My parents thought we would register again at the city hall of my hometown the next time we would go to France. My mother was at that time the deputy mayor and had the authority to marry me. However, a few months after our wedding some French colleagues at French International School advised me to register at the French Consulate, citing security purpose as the main reason. I regrettably listened to them and a few weeks later the mayor of my home town was informed that I got married in Hong Kong. My parents must have been disappointed. I think it might have been very touching to have my wedding officiated by my mother.

Living in Hong Kong

Yan and I lived at Mammy's place for six months. During this period, Mammy was the one to prepare the dinner for us. She did not want me to do any household chores. We could not communicate with each other but everything went smoothly. Every week she bought a new bouquet of chrysanthemums for our bedroom. At first I was surprised because, as with many French, I associated chrysanthemum with the cemeteries, but later I started to like these flowers.

The wet market

Yan's mum did not want me to go to the market. Although it was within walking distance from her home, she said it was too hot, the sidewalks were slippery and dirty, and it was dangerous. The street was crowded with double-parked vehicles and delivery trucks. In addition, I did not know how to buy. However, I went sometimes there by myself just to watch.

From "Easy Prosperity" building I turned left and

I walked two blocks in the direction of Admiralty. At the junction of Johnston Road and Wanchai Road I took the pedestrian crossing on my left and the street market was a little further away on my right. Everything was different from that in France and fascinating: the products, the displays, the atmosphere, and the colours. The most used unit of measurements was the Hong Kong catty (equivalent to 634g) and some fruits were sold by the British pound. Vegetables were less expensive but apples, oranges, and pears were more expensive than in France and were sold per piece. The merchants were so fast at weighing vegetables on their balance scales! The latter had only one plate and a rod. I could hardly see the plate stabilising before it immediately went up again and the vegetables were taken off!

Food markets were open every day and all day long, except on the first days of Lunar New Year. In France, street markets were usually held once or twice a week and only in the morning. Fresh vegetables and fruits, meat and fish, were

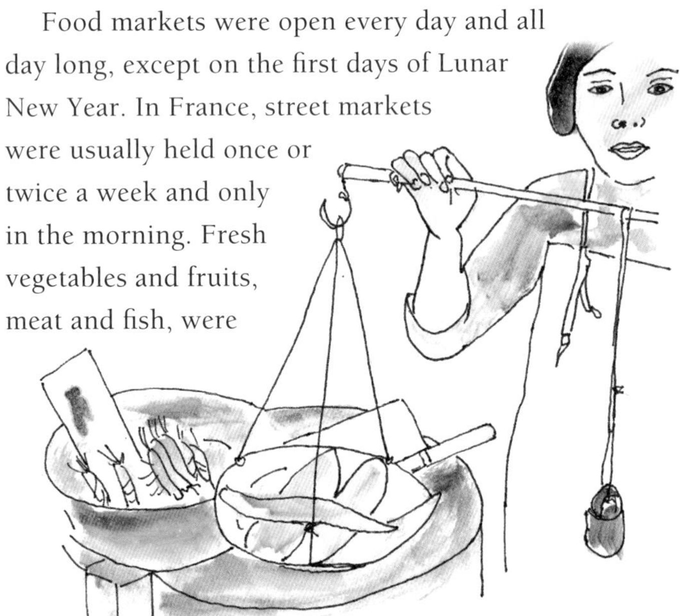

Impressed by merchants using balance scales

part of the "wet market". The "wet" name was really appropriate. Fruits and vegetables merchants never ceased watering their goods to make them look fresh. It was said that it was also a trick to make the products weigh more. Mammy was right: the sidewalks were wet with the dirty water discharged by the sellers and I had to be careful where I put my feet. The fishmongers' area was particularly slippery. Stands were lit with red lampshades to accentuate the freshness of the products and attract customers. Further up was the dry market with clothes, toys, accessories, and other merchandises.

There were heaps of green leafy vegetables and gourds that I had never seen, the red carrots were very big, and there were also green carrots. Some stalls were specialised in selling dried ingredients like red dates, white figs, snow fungus, apricot kernels, dried longans, etc. There was a stall specialised in bean curd products where you could find fresh bean sprouts and other strange stuffs like small crumpled balls and yellowish sheets. I looked at these in bewilderment. The tofu I saw in the supermarket in Paris and thought it was cheese was there too!

The butchers' stalls were also surprising. There were more pork butchers than beef butchers. Meat was hung on metal hooks. There was neither fridge nor ice-refrigerated tables. Amazingly enough, despite the heat there was no fly. It was common to see butchers smoking or having a cigarette stuck behind their ear. There was no tag indicating prices and names for the different cuts. This was really confusing for a French person. In France, each cut had a specific name stated clearly on a tag together with the cost per kg, and the meat was put on refrigerated bench. Hygiene standard was high and butchers were qualified and holding a certificate. Here, buyers simply indicated how they intended to cook the meat (in soup, stir-fry, or stew), and either the weight or the amount in HKD[16] needed. With great speed the piece was first selected, sliced on a warped chopping block, and swiftly packed in a plastic bag.

Butchers' stalls

I was amazed by the way the goods were displayed, especially the eggs stacked in a pyramid shape. Sellers knew how to use every square inch and not to waste any space, as it was limited. Hardware stores and drugstores were worth a visit. Goods were both inside and outside, on the ground, on the shelves, and hung on poles from the ceiling. It reminded me of a very old hardware shop in the town where my parents lived with stuffs filling every nook and cranny. The shop was not small at all but the owners – although not Chinese – carried so many items that they were piled to the ceiling. This shop would have fit in very well in Hong Kong.

Later I found out a stall on Argyle Street selling vegetables, fruits, and produce that were not commonly sold elsewhere. Whenever I was near Mongkok, I went there to buy vegetables. This is how I discovered mouse melon, fresh mustard tuber, bracken ferns, lotus pods, dracontomelon, etc. I would ask the seller or one of my friends to explain to me how to cook them. Then, I would introduce these vegetables on my blog together with photos and recipes.

Causeway Bay

During the first six months when we lived at Yan's mum's place, I spent a lot of time in Causeway Bay. This was a chic and fashionable area and where the monthly rentals were one of the most expensive in the world. My sisters-in-law loved shopping in this neighbourhood and I accompanied them on Saturday afternoons. I discovered the favourite pastime of Hongkongers: shopping. The four large Japanese department stores: Mitsukoshi, Sogo, Daimaru, and Matsuzakaya were located in this neighbourhood. These department stores had bakeries with very good bread. Whenever I craved for French bread during the 13 years I lived on Hong Kong Island, I went there to buy a French baguette.

Hong Kong was for sure a shopping paradise. Low-end products were juxtaposed with luxury goods. I had never seen such a high concentration of shops. People went shopping to escape from home, to have fun with their friends, to enjoy the air-conditioning and of course they made purchases too. Some also shopped to overcome stress, a common inclination in this city.

Causeway Bay was also the area to go for exercise, movies, and a good coffee. We used to run on the sports track and played tennis in Victoria Park, while others were doing Tai Chi early in the morning. In the 90s Tai Chi was getting fashionable in France and some of my friends who were taking lessons were surprised that I never learnt Tai Chi in Hong Kong yet. It was not before 2004 that I took group lessons, first on my own, then with Yan. Despite the language difficulty, I managed to remember the postures as well as their funny names such as "needle at sea bottom", "part the wild horse's mane", etc.

At that time we used to watch movies either at "The Palace" or "Lee Theatre". The cinemas had only one screen and thus were showing only one movie. The movies were shown at the same times every day. The large room was divided into smoking and smoke-free zones and there was a balcony. Outside hawkers were selling hot snacks. The curry fish balls did not bother me but the stinky tofu did. It smelled worse than an old Camembert cheese! Like durian, some say that once you have overcome its odour you would become a fan. I only tried it once many years later in a restaurant in Shanghai but have not become addicted to it. Upon leaving the theatre, the floor was covered with food wrappings and during the Lunar New Year festival, it seemed we were walking on a red carpet because of the quantity of discarded watermelon seeds on the floor. I remember watching my first Cantonese movie "A Better Tomorrow", a Hong Kong-style gangster movie, with Chow Yun-fat and Leslie Cheung starring, two excellent and charming male actors.

On Sunday afternoons we liked to go to our favourite coffee shop in Cleveland Street. An overhead sign representing an ancient coffee pot was hung above the entrance door. At that time, most of the hotels and restaurants were serving coffee powder but this small and cosy place made coffee with freshly ground beans. Although their drinks were not as strong as the espresso I was used to drinking in France, they were tasty. We liked to try different blends and chat in comfortable armchairs with our friends.

In the evening Causeway Bay was a very lively area too and it was common to see long queues at bus stops in front of Mitsukoshi on Hennessy Road even after 10 p.m. Hawkers were temporarily selling cheap clothes, electronic gadget, and street food in front of the stores. One vendor was doing brisk business selling egg-waffles and the smell of his homemade dessert attracted customers. Another vendor was busy scraping a wok full of roasted chestnuts. The view of the chestnuts reminded me of the autumn evenings when my mum roasted chestnuts on top of the oil-burner stove. The difference here was that chestnuts were not incised and when you cracked the peel open, the hot air inside suddenly escaped and could burn you. I am talking from experience!

The shop shutters were all covered with advertisings and announcements. Every evening a man was selling Chinese paintings at the same place. Next to him another merchant was selling posters of chubby babies, some with blue eyes and blonde hair. His customers were future mothers and grand-mothers who hoped that the future baby would look like the little darling on the poster they were going to put up at their homes. This made me smile.

My first typhoon

In the later summer of 1986 I experienced my first typhoon. When I heard the news that a tropical cyclone was approaching, I started to worry. The no. 1 signal had just been issued. It was hot and stuffy; there was no wind and it did not rain. Yan made me believe for a moment that we had to take refuge in the basement of the building. After my insistent questions, he reassured me: No, we only had to be careful. The greatest risk was to receive a sign or a tree branch on the head. Yes, there were trees in the city! There were also parasite trees called banyans with amazing aerial roots, some very old growing out of outdoor walls on Queens' Road in Wanchai and Hollywood Road in Central.

We put adhesive tape in form of a cross on the window panes to prevent glass splinters hurting us in case they crashed. We also made sure we had enough food for the following day in case the typhoon moved slowly.

In the evening the no. 8 signal was hoisted. We all stayed home and watched TV in the safety of our home. The wind whistling sporadically and the rain splashing against the windows were the only reminder that a typhoon was approaching. At night the roar of the wind woke me up a few times but I got back to sleep very quickly. Early in the morning Mammy was watching TV to see when the typhoon warning would be lowered to level no. 3 so she could go to work. Facing a typhoon was after all easier than I thought.

First job and commuting

In August 1986 I got my Hong Kong Identity Card and therefore was in no hurry to find a job. If I did not find one, I could study again. I enquired at the University of Hong Kong if there was any possibility of enrolling in a Master of Fines Arts programme but my visit was unfruitful as my higher diploma had no equivalence.

I realised that most of the French universities were unknown here. Should I visit the French International School (FIS) and make myself known? They might need an Arts teacher? A friend of Yan's eldest sister's used to work there and she advised me to visit the school. The FIS was in a chic and residential area on the hills of Jardines' Lookout above Causeway Bay and Tai Hang. I took the bus 11 and sat on the upper deck to admire the scenery from the top. I passed by beautiful villas with cars parked in front of large porches and high metal gates protecting the residents from prying eyes. This was a remarkable change from Wanchai and its crowded apartment buildings.

I got off at the terminus and took the first road on my left. The school building was at the end of Price Road. From there the view of Kowloon was spectacular. My interview went well and I was offered a post to supervise pupils during lunch and break times. It was not exactly what I would have liked and it was a part-time job but I accepted it hoping to get an arts teaching post later. Yan supported me. Being in contact with my fellow countrymen was more important than having a job.

Buses

The first month I worked at French International School, Mammy accompanied me to the bus stop on Hennessy Road close to the British Council. Mammy made sure that I had enough small change before leaving me. She worked in a factory in Aberdeen and was taking another bus further up the road. I put the exact fare in a box close to the bus driver. No change or ticket was given. Bus stops had no name so I made sure I knew where to get off. I could ask the passengers or the bus driver for help but they did not always answer. Either they did not speak English or they did not understand my Cantonese.

Taking taxi

After my morning job at the French International School, I gave extra-curricular ceramic and modelling classes at the German Swiss International School. There was no direct bus from Price Road to Guildford Road and I had to hurry to get there on time. I had no other choice but to take a taxi. It was easy to find a taxi in the city, except when it was raining and when they changed shift, but in this residential area I had to wait for a long time. The fare was reasonable. I can't remember the exact starting price, but definitely more affordable than in France. I either walked to Mount Butler Road, which had more traffic, or asked the school guardian to phone a taxi call centre for me. There was a surcharge of 5 HKD but at least I would get a cab and be on time.

Each time, once in the taxi I had to repeat several times my destination to the driver until he understood me. A mispronounced character meant something else. On rare occasions it happened that the taxi driver could speak a little English. Yan always told me to repeat and not to be discouraged when people did not understand what I said. Perseverance was the key! I was always wondering if I would be driven to the right place, thus, a taxi ride was stressful and not my preferred mode of transport.

Taking the elevator at "Easy Prosperity"

After work I would return home. Yan often reminded me to be cautious when taking the elevator. Before calling the lift, I used to borrow the guardian's analogue landline which was prominently on the table at the disposal of the residents to call home and see if someone could come down to pick me up. Local communications were free. Subscribers only paid a monthly fee for the rental of the device. Shop owners also had their phones put in evidence so their clients could easily use them. When nobody was answering my call, I would press on the three lifts' "up" buttons. Thus, if I did not want to go up with someone whom I did not like to be with, I could pretend that I was waiting for the other elevator.

Otherwise I would wait for Yan at the McDonald's in the CC Wu Building. It was not that I liked much the coffee there, but I could stay and read for a long time after I finished my drink. In France, the price of a cup of coffee allowed me to sit for one or two hours during which the server could not ask me to order another drink, but here even if I had stayed longer, I don't think anybody would have asked me to consume again.

A few differences

There were a few differences, whether cultural or non-cultural, between French and Hongkongers. Some of them affected me more than others, like the air-conditioning temperature being set very low or people pressing the close door button in lifts. Others did not disturb me, like using an umbrella on a sunny day or admiring pale skin. But there were also similarities between French and Hongkongers when it came to food and family values.

I was surprised by the way people were addressing and greeting each other. Yan had many names. His secondary school classmates called him Fei-zai or "fat boy" as he used to be fatty when he was younger. His other new nickname was "the Parisian". His eldest sisters called him "little brother" and his little sisters "big brother". He also had an English name but only his colleagues used it. When I first heard them referring to him as Stephen, I did not feel like they were talking about him. Similarly it took me time to get used to being called "lou-po", which literally means old and old woman. I was now his old lady! Yan became my old man or "lou-gung". I got used to hearing the word "gweilo", the slang term for Caucasians which also referred to foreigners in general, and did not find it insulting. I could not greet Yan's friends with kisses on the cheeks like we do in France. I was used to two kisses in Lyon then to four in Paris, and now none. Hongkongers greeted gweilos with a "hello" which sounded like "ha-lo" and left with a "bye-bye" with a Cantonese drawl.

I learnt not to take something literally. The first time when I heard Yan's buddies say: "Let's go yum-cha!" I took them seriously and was surprised when 10 days later they had not contacted us. Then I realised this was the equivalent of the French expression: "Let's call each other!" Another time I was taken aback when someone asked me if I had already had my lunch when it was already 3 p.m. I did not know how to reply. Later I knew that it was just a greeting or a way to start a conversation, like French people when they talk about the weather.

The air-conditioners were always set excessively low. Even in winter, public places and offices had the air-conditioners on. When I asked why, people always replied that it was to ventilate rooms and bring fresh air to avoid the spread of viruses. How wrong I was thinking that the cold air would make me sick! Then, I took the habit of carrying a jacket or a scarf to protect myself from getting cold.

People were always in a rush and very efficient. They could not wait for the lift doors to close automatically and had to hurry near the gangplank to be the first to embark and disembark from the ferry. There was always a sense of urgency in the air. I had never seen a French person pressing on the close button in the elevator. Just by watching how tables were cleared at restaurants I could tell they were quick and well-organised. All the stores, small or big, were open every day. This would have been unthinkable in France. Shop owners had to give their employees at least two rest days per week and, at that time, most of the shops in small towns were closed Sunday and Monday and during lunch time. I realised why Hongkongers always said that my birth country is a romantic place. The quality of life was for sure not as good here as in France and factory workers did not have a lot of holidays. Hongkongers were hard-working and worked long hours but also knew how to relax and enjoy foot, body, and head massage. The first time I had a haircut, I was surprised to have my hair washed on a reclining chair. I also had hair conditioner (at no extra cost) and a head massage! It was very enjoyable but wondered if this was a special treatment for me. Not at all! It was a common practice in Hong Kong. At that time, in France, you sat on a straight and uncomfortable chair with your head pulled back to have your hair washed; you had to pay for hair conditioner and there was no head massage. There were lots of massage places in Wanchai and everywhere in town, though of different standings, and having a massage in Hong Kong was very popular.

Hongkongers loved brand name items and gadgets. French, brands and products with logos were very popular. Some people were asking me how much it cost in France, thinking that every French woman had her brand bag. Spending a fortune for a handbag decorated with initials or a brand watch to show my status: not for me! But there were lots of fakes which they were very fond of too!

I was surprised, and at the same time found it embarrassing to see people admiring gweilos' pale skin and tall noses. Hongkongers liked the gweilos' white skin and whitening cosmetic products were in high-demand. This was hard to understand for me as French were proud of having a sun-tanned complexion; it showed that they had been skiing or sunbathing on a Mediterranean beach. Here, it was the opposite. A pale skin was chic and dark-skinned people were looked down upon and presumed to have come from China and worked in a rice field. Not only did women lighten their skin and put sunscreens on to protect it from the harmful rays, but they also opened their umbrella as soon as the sun showed its face. This made me smile. Was it because of these habits that Hong Kong ladies all looked younger than their age? At that time French people were not very mindful of the harmful effects of the sun on the skin.

At one time I thought of buying a pretty white lace sun umbrella I had seen at Yue Wah in Causeway Bay, but it could not be folded and would have been unpractical to be carried around. Thus, I started to use an umbrella too! Not only Hongkongers were admiring the pale skin of gweilos but also the height of their nose. How many times I heard that my nose was tall! I always thought that it was long. One thing was sure, Chinese liked the bridge-like nose that separated gweilos' eyes and did not like to have a flat nose. Nobody was pleased with what Mother Nature had given them!

Hongkongers seldom entertained at home and ate a lot outside. With so many restaurants and the small size of the apartments, it was understandable. To prepare a Chinese meal also required good timing and organisation so that the several dishes and the soup were all served at once. It was easier to prepare a western meal.

It was very important for Chinese to show that they had enough to eat. Yan could not appreciate that I would eat freshly baked bread after dinner in front of everyone in the minibus. It looked like he did not have enough money to buy a meal for his wife. It was also polite to greet someone with a "you have put on weight!" which was for a French woman pretty embarrassing. I recall Kau-mou and Gau-yi, Yan's aunties, meeting me and saying loudly in front of everyone how I looked fatter than before. Chinese parents liked chubby kids as it showed they could provide enough food to their family, a sign of prosperity. However, contrary to most French people, Hongkongers did not seem to like sweets a lot. There were a few pastry shops but the cakes did not attract me. They looked too artificial with their colourful whipping cream. I remember my first and only time when I made a chocolate cake for some friends. Hardly anyone touched it. People were health conscious and it was simply too rich. I was so disappointed. My father would not have minded to eat half of it all by himself!

And, as I mentioned before, people were more conservative in terms of clothing. Yan was getting more traditional than in Paris and did not want me to wear low-neckline clothes or tank tops that were more revealing than what locals preferred.

What I missed

I missed my parents, my friends, French songs, cafés, long daylights, lively conversations, quiet places, and exhibitions. But there were many good points in Hong Kong that counterbalanced what I was missing. Transportation, safety, convenience, efficiency, effervescence, and a breath-taking harbour made up for the just as bad summer heat, humidity, and crowded places. I sometimes felt nostalgic but it did not last long.

Before coming to Hong Kong I had lived in Nanterre for three years, far away from my parents. I had learnt to be independent and was used to not seeing them often. When leaving France I told them that I would write regularly but over the years I wrote less and less, but phoned more and more. Thanks to the decreasing cost of communication over the years, we will call each other more often and talk for longer time. Over the years I have also felt more need to phone and listen to the voice of my parents. Later, I have also sent emails as my dad became computer literate at the age of 68.

Because of the language it was difficult to make new pals. I was missing my friends, especially my best girlfriend and confidant. When I went back to Lyon in

1987, she was working abroad and we did not see each other. When I returned again in 1991, not only was I married but I had a 15-month-old baby! Although we wrote to each other during those 5 ½ years, there was a lot of catching up. I recalled that she made fun of me when I mentioned a pop singer who was no longer in this world and did not know the name of a certain band. I badly needed to update my records!

We went to karaoke with Yan's friends but the songs were not the same. Jean-Jacques Goldman, Étienne Daho, or Telephone, were far away. Besides the Beatles' songs (Hongkongers loved this group!), I did not know the English songs that they liked to sing such as the Carpenters', and I could not read the Chinese characters of the Chinese songs. In addition, the lyrics were in literary Cantonese which was not the same as spoken Cantonese. Canto-pop was in full wave. By dint of hearing the same songs over and over again, I got to recognise the chorus of some of them, such as "Monica" by Leslie Cheung and "Break the iceberg" by Anita Mui, and could sing along.

I was lost in translation. Yan and his buddies rarely spoke English amongst themselves and when it happened they returned quickly to their mother tongue which I completely understood and accepted. I would not imagine French people speaking English among themselves. Hong Kong was a British colony, but except for a few luxury lifestyle magazines and foreign editions of fashion magazines, there was no English language tabloid, weekly, or magazine on local arts and culture. On one hand it was good because I saved money, but on the other hand when the conversation turned to the life of celebrities and local socialites, as inevitably it happened, I felt left out. I was, like everybody else, curious. Thus, I was eager to learn Cantonese as I wanted to understand what people were saying around me and be able to better appreciate the local culture. People did not talk much about politics. The economy was doing very well and unemployment was virtually non-existent. I recalled the heated discussions during family gatherings in France. It was both entertaining and scary for us, the kids, to see the adults passionately expressing their views and raising their voices. It was not the time for us to say anything. I read the English-language newspapers and listened to the English radio to keep abreast of the news. There was not much news about my country – the social and political issues of my country did not make the headlines in Hong Kong. How much different my life would have been if I had had Internet. Besides, I noticed that the English-language newspapers were not always covering the same news as the Chinese-language newspapers.

Besides the remote places we crossed when hiking, it was hard to find peaceful areas in the city especially at weekends. It was impossible to be the only one walking in the street. I recall when I returned to France after one year in Hong Kong and realised there was no one in front of and behind me. It was lunch time, the shops were closed and the street was deserted! I thought something was wrong.

During my free time, I went to the art museum in City

Hall to see Chinese porcelains but for sure the Guimet Museum in Paris had a bigger collection – of course some were from China. I was interested in ceramics but there were not many exhibitions of local ceramicists' works and fewer exhibitions of young artists' works and artistic performances here than in Paris. But art and culture were all around me. I was busy discovering and enjoying new food and different types of eateries. I liked the atmosphere of dai-pai-dong (popular restaurants), cha-chaan-teng (Hong Kong-style café), and traditional Cantonese restaurants. The dim sum culture must have had some influences on the new cuisine as seen by the future trend of mini-dishes and elegant style, against traditional cooking and hearty meals.

I often went to Victoria Park and observed the elderly men walking their birds or playing go. Early in the morning people were doing Tai Chi exercises. I visited wet markets and streets specialised in printing, sheet metal fabrication, markets specialised in gold fish, flowers, and birds. I rode the Star Ferry and the tram.

I missed the atmosphere of French cafés. I always loved the aroma of coffee and entering a café was comforting and bringing back memories. I remember the coffee roaster's shop when I was little and asking my mum to stop for a while so I could smell the freshly roasted coffee beans scent. Coffee aroma was also associated with my student life and the lunch breaks when my classmates and I would go to a café to chat and play pinballs. After moving to Chi Fu Fa Yuen at the end of 1986, I discovered a French-style café bakery in World

Pleasurable tram rides

Wide Plaza in Central. At that time there were not many coffee houses, unlike today when they are sprouting everywhere! I liked to go there for a cup of coffee but it was more for the comforting smell and the memories than the taste of the beverage itself.

One thing, however, that I was not missing was the feeling of insecurity that I had in France. I felt more secure in Hong Kong than in Paris. The MTR was also very safe and the service more reliable than the French subways. I was afraid to take the metro at night in Paris and some lines were particularly unsafe for women. I also feared the crowd and chaotic situation whenever the employees of the Autonomous Operator of Parisian Transports were on strikes, drastically cutting down the number of operating trains. To be fair, the Hong Kong MTR had long and narrow platforms, so jam-packed that I could not move. It was common to wait for a couple of trains before I could board because of the commuter crush. But Hongkongers were used to crowds. They were orderly and boarding and alighting were never wildly chaotic!

The streets were safer too. I have never felt threatened when walking in the street. In France it was also common to get whistled at by construction workers when passing in front of construction sites. While some women might feel insulted and others pleased, I felt it was like being harassed. Luckily it did not happen to me often. I have never heard girls being wolf-whistled in Hong Kong. Were Chinese men more respectful towards women or were they shy? But I knew that crimes happened too here and had been shocked by the killing of two young foreigners in Braemar Hill[17]. The presence of security guards in buildings, banks, and jewellery stores, although not a perfect deterrent, was also a reminder of potential burglaries.

Yan's family was my new family, and his sisters, though very discreet, were always there if I needed them. Mammy was unobtrusive too and very kind. Whenever I said she was wearing something nice, she would buy the same clothes for me. I could not tell her in a diplomatic way, in my broken Cantonese, that it was lovely but not my style nor for my age.

I particularly missed my parents on Christmas day when the whole family had a warm and lively lunch together, a gathering similar to the Chinese New Year's Eve dinner, but with gifts and the traditional turkey and Christmas cake. Adults stayed at the table for hours chatting and drinking (of course!). When the conversation turned to politics, generally near the end of the meal, and after we had my mum's chestnut purée and chocolate Yule log, it was time for us, kids, to go and play in our bedrooms, and let the adults have their heated debate. The funniest Christmas I had in Hong Kong was when my parents came in 1997. The bird flu was hitting Hong Kong and my mum had brought us a fresh turkey from one of her distant relatives, as well as wine and papillotes[18] in her suitcase. However, the luggage did not arrive with them and we were anxious if we would be able to get it for our dinner. Luckily, everything was delivered on time and nothing was lost.

During our dinner we kept laughing at the bird's long trip in my parents' luggage. We also had an interesting Christmas Eve with lots of sweets and little dishes due to my bad organisational skills. Each of our friends was supposed to contribute a dish but they all brought a dessert!

I also wished my parents were with me at barbecue parties. When the weather was cooler in winter, Yan's friends loved to go to the country parks where places were equipped with barbecue pits, tables, and benches. In France, barbecues were done at home, and in my family my mum would season the meat while my dad was in charge of grilling it. I never had to do anything but enjoy the food. Everyone had to season his/her own meat and prick it on forks. I also had no patience to sit and watch the meat being cooked, and in my case, getting burnt. For sure the Hong Kong-style barbecues were very entertaining and enjoyable on cool and refreshing winter days, but it would be even better if my parents were with us.

Lucien's birth

At the end of 1989 a new chapter in my life started. I was expecting a baby and in a few months' time I would be a mother. It was exciting. I became the prime attention of Yan and his mum until our baby's first month. Afterwards, I was still well taken care of but our son became the centre of our life. We had employed a full-time domestic helper so I would not have to do any house chores. What Yan had told me back in 1983 came true.

Yan and Mammy were very happy and made sure that I was eating the proper food. I had never heard French women being advised on what they should or should not eat during their pregnancy. Western doctors gave you supplements and told you to drink milk and eat a balanced diet. Here it was not my doctor – he was British – but Mammy who was telling me to avoid eating hot and spicy food such as tropical fruit. These would give too much heat and dampness in my body thus unbalancing my body constitution. Mammy also said that I should avoid drinking coffee. This had nothing to do with traditional Chinese medicine but she believed that the black drink will darken the baby's skin. Was it a myth? It might not darken the skin but might affect the baby's weight. I drank less coffee and I can testify that our baby had a beautiful pale skin.

My parents were very happy too but were too far to give me much advice. My mother who had come to Hong Kong a few months earlier warned me to sit down properly on the bus and hold on the back of the seat in front of me or grab a pole. She could not forget our bumpy rides on Chi Fu Road!

Lucien was born four days before the scheduled date. The day before, one of my colleagues had brought me green beans from her garden. It was rare to find such extra fine beans in Hong Kong and I had a lot. During the night I was awakened by a bellyache and I thought that I had too many beans, but Yan reminded me that the birth of our baby was approaching so we left home for the hospital quickly. Even in the middle of the night it was easy to find a taxi.

During my pregnancy Yan and I attended prenatal classes. The nurses told us about the Chinese tradition that dictates women to stay at home during the first month following birth and not to take a shower or wash their hair. The Chinese believed that water penetrated through the pores of the skin and made it more difficult to convalesce. However, the nurses also told us that it was no longer reasonable to observe this custom because we had hot water and hairdryers at home. They also joked about it and said that if we did not take a shower, they would not come in our room to take care of us. It made sense! So I took a shower just after Lucien's birth and I did not wait for one month before going out.

Mammy did not stay with us during the one-month post-natal confinement. We had a full-time domestic helper and I already felt that we did not have any privacy anymore.

It was not easy to take care of a baby and I did not know why he was crying. It was particularly annoying when he started crying in the evening when Yan was home. When Lucien was sleeping, I did not have much to do, but I was afraid of leaving him alone and did not know where to go. I would have liked to be in France with my family but it was not possible as Lucien was too small to travel.

I had chosen a Christian name for our son and Yan had yet to give him a Chinese name. According to the tradition we had to use a generation name which was already set and just choose another character. But Mammy, who was quite superstitious, sought a geomancer's advice and the latter advised us to forfeit the generation name and proposed to us two new characters: "Pou" and "Gim". "Pou" was one of the characters for dandelion and also a Chinese drug used in Traditional Chinese Medicine. "Gim" meant "sword". Thus the combination of the name "Pou-gim" symbolised lightness and protection against illness, as well as firmness. This has been a good choice.

Mammy and Lucien

Recovery food

Chinese people were very knowledgeable about nutrition before and after pregnancy, so women could recover well. When I was expecting Lucien, I learnt about the harmful effects of some food and learnt that I had to avoid "heaty" food. According to traditional Chinese medicine, tropical fruits like longan, mango, banana, and durian were too hot and said to bring heat and dampness, hence not good during pregnancy. I could go without durian without any problem. Mammy loved it and tried on several occasions to convince me to have a bite. However, it was so stinky that I could not swallow it. A few years later I tried it again with sweetened glutinous rice and it tasted better than it smelled.

Then, after Lucien's birth, I had to strengthen my convalescent body. Mammy brought me a fresh slaughtered chicken almost every day to make into a soup. To celebrate her grand-son's first month, Mammy cooked pig's trotters and ginger in black vinegar for us and also gave some to family members and friends. This was the same dark beverage my Hong Kong girlfriend whom I met in Paris made me drink almost four years ago. This iron-rich dish was also supposed to energise me. The sauce was very dark and the white of the hard-boiled eggs had turned black and did not look appetising. However, I liked the strong ginger-flavoured sauce.

I also consumed essence of chicken, another strange black beverage that some relatives had offered me. This very nourishing tonic was also supposed to accelerate my physical recovery. It had a very strong taste, not at all like chicken. I did not like it but drank all the little bottles as these were not cheap and I could not waste them. Other relatives had offered me birds' nest soup, another fortifier. The delicacy was presented in small glass jars. This tonic was comparatively very easy to drink, sweet with some crunchy bits.

But the strangest of all the tonics I had to drink was a soup that I made with frog ovaries that Yan's second eldest sister had brought me. I soaked this delicacy and herbal medicine in water overnight and then double-steamed it, same as for a bird's nest soup, for several hours so as to keep all its essence and moisture. I cannot recall how the "double-steamed snow frog" tasted like, but I remember that I had added rock sugar to sweeten it and help me swallow it! But again it was supposed to be good for my condition and I drank it all. When I mentioned this to my parents, they were astonished and looked at me with a disgusted expression.

When I looked back at this part of my life, I think it was not easy to give birth but it was a worthwhile experience.

Care and education

In September, after my maternity leave and the school summer holiday I resumed my job. Yan and I asked Mammy to take care of Lucien and she was more than happy. Four eyes (the maid's and hers) were better than two (only the maid's). She was not 60 years old yet but had stopped working the previous year, as most of her children were now supporting the family. Unlike in France, there was no retirement pension and traditionally children were taking care of their elderly parents.

Mammy was looking after Lucien very well but not always the way I would have wanted. I did not like my son to eat dim sum too often – I believed there was too much Mono Sodium Glutamate (MSG) – nor to choose his food. I would have liked him to sit down and learn how to eat properly, the way I was brought up. Mammy would not mind chasing after him to feed him, but although she did that he did not eat better. I was worried Lucien would become a "child-king" or I should say a "little-emperor".

It was difficult for Yan to contradict and give directives to his mum. She was helping us and we are already very grateful. For sure, the way the French educated their children was very different from the Chinese and at that time it was difficult to know which one would work better. For example, I never succeeded in putting Lucien to bed early. Most of the kids in Hong Kong stayed up very late and parents did not have any evening for themselves. Parenting was quite tiring and by listening to my cousin in France it seemed it was much easier for her to be a mother than for me.

My friends and relatives in France were stunned to learn that it was common to see young couples in Hong Kong with their maid in tow at restaurant on Sunday. Like them, I would have felt awkward to have someone else feeding my son while I only had the weekend to take

Ah-gung, Ah-po, and Lucien

care of him. But one thing I conceded was that I asked my helper to feed him at night. Other parents were doing the same, and they told me that the helper could wake up at night, because she could take a rest during day time but I could not. I could not understand why most babies in France could sleep through the nights but my baby could not.

These differences in education gradually disappeared over the years when Lucien grew up.

When Lucien was big enough to go to school, we started considering whether it was better to enrol him in a local school or an international school. But when I heard parents whose children went to local schools complaining about spending their whole evenings helping their children with their homework, I knew I would be useless when it came to Chinese subjects, so we opted for an English curriculum. Lucien spoke French and Cantonese at home. In fact he knew how to speak Cantonese before French. I remember him asking me why I was speaking French to him. Everybody was praising his fluency in Chinese and English and he thought he was Chinese and English. Later when Lucien was six years old and I was working at French International School, we went to my parents' place every summer and Lucien learnt more French very quickly. He switched easily between the three languages and knew which one to use with whom: Cantonese with his dad and grand-mother, French with me, and English at school.

Hongkongers had two attitudes when it came to

education. They were very protective; for example they did not let their kids touch dirty things and were spoiling them. But in terms of school education, they were very pushy and filled their kids' schedules with many types of extra-curricular activities. Our son only learnt to play violin and write Chinese characters, the latter because he was forced to by his dad. Lucien thanks his dad today for having forced him to learn Chinese when he was small. I must add that he had a big incentive: he was receiving a lai see[19] from his grand-mother each time he had full marks, and he got many! Did he have enough activities? Did that make him less competitive than his peers? I don't think so. Today I recall that I was afraid that Lucien would be too spoiled and not respect us. I was wrong, and I realised that the most important thing was to show him family values. What he experienced with his grand-mother in Hong Kong and grand-parents in France are invaluable. Yan and I successfully instilled in him family values and our son grew up to be a kind and well-intentioned young man.

Settling down

During my first visit in Hong Kong in 1985, I saw the city with a tourist's eye although I did not consider myself one and did not have enough time to imagine how my life would be when I came back one year later.

This time I was discovering with fun and excitement the daily life of Hongkongers. The city was an amazing place, full of vitality, convenient, and where I felt safe and it was like I was on holiday. I liked the liveliness of the city and its illuminated signs in streets and skyscrapers at night and the proximity of the sea and country parks. It was easy to adapt as Yan was always here to explain me things and smooth out every little bump that I could encounter in my daily life.

For sure my five senses had been awakened with new odours, writings, faces, climate, languages, and flavours. I also became aware of a different way of thinking and superstitious practices.

Time was flying and three years passed. Although we said when I came in 1986 that we would consider whether or not to move back to France three years later, we did not have to think twice. Yan had started his career and I liked Hong Kong so there was no point in starting all over again in France. I had settled down and decided to make Hong Kong my adopted country.

Although I felt comfortable in Hong Kong, I had to find my bearings each time when we moved to a new area. Yan and I moved eight times in 30 years and lived in seven districts! Each time I had to get used to new supermarkets, stores, and wet markets. I also had to find out where the shoemaker, the stationery shop, and photo printing service were located.

After 10 years on Hong Kong Island, we moved to Kowloon Tong where we had lived for 13 years, and then to Fo Tan where we had stayed for four years and finally to Tai Po where we are today. I have lived in very densely populated areas and more deserted places, in high-rises and lately in an individual house; in the city, the suburbs, and today in the countryside.

Our first home

At the end of 1986, almost six months after getting married, we moved out of Mammy's home. Yan's eldest sister was planning to move back with Mammy and she suggested us to rent the flat she was going to vacate in Chi Fu Fa Yuen. She also proposed to leave her furniture to us. We visited her apartment in the Pok Fu Lam area, at the southwest side of Hong Kong Island. The residential complex of Chi Fu Fa Yuen reminded me of "City One" in Shatin, although on a smaller scale and airier. It had only 20 towers of 28 storeys each. Each block formed an eight-branch cross. On each floor four apartments were distributed on both sides of a central landing. We liked the flat and the location suited us too. We accepted Yan's eldest sister's proposal and moved there. From the 18th floor of our block we could see Lamma Island's power station and its two coal towers.

After living on our own, Yan did the cooking and I was doing the laundry and tidying up. The kitchen was small. I had to hang out the washing on sliding nylon strings between two outside walls, between our kitchen and the neighbour's kitchen. To access the cloth line, I had to squeeze myself between the washing machine and the kitchen sink and lean through the window. This space was not ventilated enough and in spring the humidity level was so high that clothes took time to dry and smelled musty. No wonder there were so many

Pok Fu Lam Village

laundries in the city. Their service was cheaper and faster than in France. You could bring your washing and have it cleaned within a few hours. In spring, the humidity was such that mould was growing under the sole of our shoes, on leather bags and belts and it was impossible to get rid of it. The building exterior walls and the floors were so slippery that the security guards put carpets in the building entrance hall to prevent people from slipping. In autumn, when warm clothes were taken out of drawers after having been squeezed for about six months, the smell of naphthalene was hard to get rid of. The seasonal mothballs scent lasted longer than an expensive perfume! Luckily later odourless mothballs were invented.

After we moved, we used to go to Mammy's place once a week for dinner. Before going back home, we used to buy a loaf of pre-sliced white bread on Hennessy Road for our breakfast. Although I was full, I could not help myself from eating some slices. Yan was not pleased, telling me that people would think that he could not afford to feed his wife with a proper meal and thus had to eat bread. I really did not care as I did not know many people. I was used to eating bread three times a day in France. Occasionally I was making my own bread, but this loaf was different with its soft inside.

We could find all the daily necessities in the commercial centre of Chi Fu Fa Yuen. There was also a convenience store which had a phone booth and before we had a line for international direct calls installed at our home, I could call my parents there. There was also a small indoor wet market. Yan was concerned that sellers would increase their prices if they saw him with a gweimui, and he asked me to stand behind him. Later, I went to the market on my own without thinking whether I was being cheated or not. I bought from the same vendors and they recognised me and sometimes gave me discounts. On weekends we had more time and walked down to the wet market in the old Pok Fu Lam village where the vegetables and fruits were cheaper. Villagers displayed their produce on the ground in front of their houses. There was an old lady selling bean curd and I tried her homemade tofu pudding. The addition of ginger syrup gave some zing to the otherwise bland fresh curds. This is how I gradually started to like tofu.

Then winter came. The air was blowing through the windows of our flat. There was no central heating. We

Eating bread on mini-bus

knew the cold would not last and we simply put on more layers of clothes. Although it was relatively warm compared to the winter in France, it felt much colder than it actually was due to the high level of humidity and the flat's bad thermal insulation.

Each day I started the day by saying good morning to the security guard. Sitting on a chair behind a table he lifted his head and greeted me in return. When I returned home in green minibus 22 to Pok Fu Lam I shouted to the driver "Please stop under the bridge!" It was much easier than taking a taxi! Strangely, there were some words that I could never say in the right order, and Yan always teased me when I wanted to say that "I was very thirsty" or "hou-hao-hot". It sounded like "hot-hao-hou" or "hot-hao-hao". It still happens today!

At that time, Yan's office was in the Argyle Centre Tower II in Sai Yeung Choi Street South in Mongkok.

Yan told me not to stand near him when paying for our shopping.

This was where City Polytechnic (which was to become City University) was located and where the Trade and Industry Department is today. I met him there many times. It was very odd to imagine students studying on top of a shopping centre next to some of the busiest shopping streets of Hong Kong. I was bewildered by the quantity of small shops selling cheap clothes, accessories, and food. People were queuing up to buy fish balls or deep-fried chicken legs in front of the stalls. Some stall holders were busy deep-frying vegetables and stinky tofu while others were grilling octopus and intestines. A flow of customers kept coming, and even during summer, groups of youngsters seemed to enjoy eating their hot and oily snack outdoor standing on the pavements. I actually never tried these snacks although it was tempting. I had a sensitive stomach and I did not dare to try. During the summer, I had received cholera vaccine as there were a few cases in Hong Kong and I often suffered bouts of diarrhoea. It was nothing serious. I was just slowly getting used to Cantonese food.

Yan and I both used public transport to go to work. Yan and I did not have a driving license and we did not have the intention to learn to drive soon as having a car in Hong Kong was very expensive. A car park space was very costly too. I recalled that in Chi Fu Fa Yuen it cost about 700 HKD per month (at the end of 1980s). We never thought one day we would have a car. Besides, public transport was very efficient and buses and mini-buses ran frequently. However, depending on the road condition, the bus rides could be bumpy. The buses that came from England were old and had no air conditioning, and their shock absorbers were worn out. I remember the rides with my mother when she came to see us for the first time in 1989. We had to hang on tight in the sharp bends of Chi Fu Road and on Pok Fu Lam Road.

In early 1990, our landlord told us that he was selling his flat for 880,000 HKD, for an approximately 500 square-feet flat. This was an exorbitant sum and we did not have enough savings to pay for the deposit so we moved. It would have been a good investment: 25 years later the same apartment cost 10 times more, and its rent had quadrupled. After having lived for 3 ½ years in Chi Fu Fa Yuen, we moved to Robinson Road.

Other homes and areas

After living in Chi Fu Fa Yuen we moved to Robinson Road in Mid-Levels. The area was getting trendier, more expensive and prestigious from day to day. New residential high-rises kept sprouting next to old buildings and blocking the view of the residents living on lower floors. Our flat was very spacious (about 1,800 square-feet), but the rent was comparatively affordable as it was an old edifice surrounded by building sites. We were also on the 18th floor and had a superb view of Victoria Harbour and Kowloon. However, very quickly our nice view disappeared as many buildings were being built all around us. Without respite, pounding and drilling sounds punctuated the day. It was very dusty and every evening Yan had to hunt mosquitoes before we went to bed. From the window of our living room, I could also follow the progress of the reclamation work of the new airport at Chek Lap Kok on Lantau and the harbour being slowly filled with soil. Mid-Levels were developing fast. At that time the longest outdoor escalator in the world was also being built. When my parents came in the summer 1992, its construction had just started and one year later they saw it in operation. This shows the efficiency of Hongkongers and how fast buildings were being erected in Hong Kong. It was said that constructors were erecting one floor per day. Every day the scenery around us was changing!

Lucien was small and at weekends we took him to Victoria Park. He liked to play ball with his dad and watch the remote-control sailboats cruising on the artificial pool. We also went to the Zoo and Botanical Gardens in Central to see the monkeys and the tiger. We also brought him to the newly opened Central Park to play on the swing and watch the birds in the immense aviary. These two places were not far away from our home and we just went there on foot. On Sunday afternoon we did our shopping at the wet markets in the narrow and steep streets in Mid-Levels. The area was unique and had village-like feel with its streets lined with traditional shops, its wet markets, and dai-pai-dongs. On our way home we liked to stop at a cha-chaan-teng (Hong Kong-style café) on Caine Road. If we were lucky, we would arrive just on time when their pineapple buns came out from the oven. Their milk tea was good too. I started to enjoy these treats almost as much as an

The longest outdoor escalator in Mid-Levels

espresso and a French croissant.

Then, in mid-1994, we moved to North-Point in the eastern part of Hong Kong. The towers of Provident Centre formed a wall along the eastern corridor and our block was trapped around high-rises. From our flat we could see the planes landing and taking off on the other side of the harbour. There was an outdoor swimming pool where Lucien learnt to swim with his dad. Yan's way to incite his son to learn swimming was to give him money each time he went to the swimming pool. The money was actually not given directly to Lucien but put into his bank account. At first I really missed the attractiveness of Mid-Levels. North-Point was very crowded but very convenient in terms of shopping and transportation. It was also not far away from Causeway Bay which I was familiar with. On weekends Lucien could still play ball with his dad in Victoria Park.

I recall that in 1992 I took the vehicular ferry to cross the harbour from North-Point to Kowloon City with my parents who had come to Hong Kong to spend their holiday with us. One of Yan's friends had picked them up at Kai Tak Airport and drove them to our home in Robinson Road. It was a novel experience for me to get off the car to enjoy the harbour view, better than crossing through the tunnel.

During the week, I was working in Hung Hom and enjoyed commuting by ferry. However, I was apprehensive in spring when the visibility was very low. I recall one morning when I was suddenly woken up from my torpor by the sound of the fog horn and saw a huge containership very close to us. Phew, we had just avoided a collision.

In 1996, after two years in North-Point, we moved to Kowloon Tong, on Kowloon Peninsula. We stayed in Kowloon Tong for 13 years during which we moved three times. At the beginning I missed the convenience, dynamism, and charm of Hong Kong Island that I had known for the past 10 years. Kowloon Tong was a residential area, and was much less crowded and had large avenues lined with trees. Sometimes I felt I was in France although there were no horse chestnut and plane trees, unlike in my country. In spring the red flowers of the cotton tree looked like big flames demarcating Cornwall Street, while the last pink-purplish orchid-like blossoms of the bauhinia trees, soon to become the city emblem, started to wilt and the bougainvillea bloomed on Tak Chee Avenue.

In our first flat, we could see the planes and hear their engine over our heads. We also heard crackling noises from our TV set whenever the jets were getting closer. Furthermore, a shopping centre next to our building was being built and it was, like back in Robinson Road, dusty, noisy, and full of mosquitoes. We used to go shopping in Kowloon City and park our car on the mall's rooftop in Carpenter Street. From there Lucien liked to watch the planes taking their turn and descending slowly onto the city making their way through the buildings. The engine noise was deafening. The closest wet market was in Nam Shan Estate in Shek Kip Mei, just behind City University, at about 15 minutes by foot from home. In late 1998,

During a ferry ride on a foggy day,
a containership suddenly loomed close.

after the closure of Kai Tak Airport and the opening of Festival Walk – at that time the biggest shopping centre in Hong Kong – our home became quieter and less dusty. There were no more planes flying over our heads and no more TV crackling noise. We also went less often to Kowloon City and did our shopping at Festival Walk, next to our home. It was very convenient and we spent a lot of time there, not only shopping but also having meals and watching movies. Nowadays we still go there from time to time, especially to watch movies.

Three years later we moved to another quarter of City University, also in Kowloon Tong. This time our building was next to a school and at weekends it was, again, very noisy. I recall when boy scouts were rehearsing and shouting at weekends during the whole afternoon: "1-2-3-1-2-3-1-2-3!"

Five years later we moved back to the first quarter where we used to live between 1996 and 1999. Lucien left in September 2006 to the United Kingdom to study and our home suddenly became very quiet. We started to hike again and walked regularly – almost every week – from Tung Chung to Tai O. It is also during that period that I resumed learning Putonghua.

In March 2009 we moved away from the Kowloon Peninsula and went to Fo Tan in the New-Territories, behind the Lion Rock tunnel. For many people living on Hong Kong Island, Kowloon seemed very far away from their home and the New-Territories seemed to be at the end of the world; thus they seldom crossed the harbour and came to this side of Hong Kong. Our flat was on a hill facing Shatin and from our balcony I could see "City One", the first residential area I visited in the New-Territories back in 1985. The view at night was beautiful. During the Tuen Ng festival we could see the dragon boat races on the Shing Mun River. The boats were too far to be seen clearly, but we could hear the distant drums' beats helping the paddlers to stay in sync with each other. I had never been particularly interested in the races but always liked the glutinous rice dumplings, a specialty that Hongkongers eat during this festival. My favourite was the savoury types with fatty pork, mung beans, and salted egg yolks. However, I had never tried to make some myself but I know that special skill is required to wrap the ingredients in bamboo leaves.

We were far from the urban area and could no longer decide to watch a movie at the last-minute. We had to plan our activities in advance and not to forget to buy anything before going back home. However, I gradually started to appreciate living in the suburbs while at the same time being able to reach the city within 10 to 15 minutes by mini-bus. Every day, I took the minibus at the bottom of our building to Pai Tau Village below Shatin train station. Upon arrival at the minibus terminus, I was greeted by the same song played by the ice-cream truck. People living in the neighbourhood used bicycles to commute to the train station and there were lots of bicycles chained to the railings nearby. I became familiar with the surroundings of Shatin train station, and particularly its shopping malls. I could find everything in this new town but did not find it any charms. The wet market in Shatin was small and Yan and I started to go to Tai Po to buy vegetables as there were a larger number of sellers.

We practised Tai Chi on the rooftop of our building, overlooking Shatin. There were lots of monkeys living in the green area above Sui Wo Road which were not afraid of coming closer to our building. There was also a nice trail which started from the end of Sui Wo Road to Tsuen Wan, but I did not like the way the monkeys standing on the road were looking at us when we walked past them.

They were particularly numerous around the Shing Mun Reservoir. For that reason, and because the hike was quite tough, with lots of stairs to climb, we preferred hiking from Tung Chung to Tai O.

After living in Fo Tan for four years we moved again in mid-2013 to Tai Po, northeast of Shatin. This time we had moved to the countryside. We were far from the city and closer to China than Wanchai. We are living in an individual house and it is the first time we are not surrounded by towers. It is very green and the air is cleaner than in Fo Tan. There are beautiful birds which sing marvellously, butterflies, frogs, and lizards, but also mosquitoes and snakes – which are my nightmare!

I knew already Tai Po Hui Market, but after moving, a friend of mine showed me other street markets and shops. I like the diversity of Tai Po. Some areas remind

Ice-cream truck outside Shatin train station

me of the Wanchai that I knew 30 years ago with small boutiques, traditional shops selling "dried delicacies from the sea and mountains", stationery and hardware stores. Frame manufacturers, glaziers, and shoemakers are still practising their trade. And one of the best things: it is convenient to buy seafood at Tai Po Hui Market and have it prepared at the Cooked Food Centre above the market. I got used to living in Tai Po and quite like it.

Having fresh steamed fish at Cooked Food Centre

Mainland China and Macau – 1986 and after

Honeymoon in Shenzhen

For our wedding gift, Yan's second eldest sister had offered us a gift voucher for two nights at the Shenzhen Bay Hotel, a brand-new hotel in Shenzhen. I knew that the border city was part of the first Chinese Special Economic Zone and therefore in full development. I got a visa at the "China Travel Services" (CTS) in Wanchai that allowed me to stay in China for one month.

This was my first trip to China. We took the cross-harbour tunnel from Wanchai to Hung Hom and from there the train to Lo Wu station, the terminus. After going through the Hong Kong Immigration, we crossed a bridge. The Shenzhen River that ran underneath had a very unpleasant smell and it was very hot. I could not see what was in front of me except people's back. I followed the crowd and kept walking forward, staying very close to Yan as I did not want to lose sight of him. We finally arrived at the Chinese border. Yan helped me to fill in my immigration card. Then we had to split up. Yan had to go to the counters for Overseas Chinese on the lower ground floor whereas I had to stay on the ground floor where the counters for foreigners were located. Yan's procedure would be faster than mine and he would wait for me at the exit. I was a little anxious as it was the first time I was alone and there were so many people queueing up. I did not understand anything. What if I could not find Yan later in the arrival hall? Phew! Luckily I found him quickly among the crowd!

The doors of the arrival hall were wide open facing a square where groups of people were gathered. Young people came toward us saying something which I did not quite understand. They were turning around us and constantly repeating what I finally caught was "change-money – change-money". They wanted to exchange Hong Kong Dollars for their local currency to allow them to buy goods that were otherwise only accessible to foreigners. We would also benefit from a better exchange rate than the official one.

The hotel was in the middle of nowhere and there was nothing special worth seeing or visiting within the hotel vicinity, but only fields and a small restaurant by the side of the road where we had steamed shrimps in the evening. After dinner we went downtown but there was nothing much of interest either.

Two days later we returned to Wanchai. Yan was still on vacation and we decided to go to China again but for a longer trip. Shenzhen was a new city and did not have much to see that was typical of China. This time we wanted to go to Xi'an.

For many years I did not feel like going back to Shenzhen although Mammy was telling me how great it was. In the early 90s she used to go there very often with her friends and spent the whole day enjoying massage and dim sum. She also liked to have clothes tailor-made there. Everything was much cheaper than in Hong Kong and like many Hongkongers she liked very much her outings to Shenzhen. It did not take her very long to go there by train and getting through the immigration was easy as she held a Home Return Permit. But I needed to apply for a visa at the border. After living in Hong Kong for seven years, I had a Permanent Identity Card and the smart card allowed me to pass through the Hong Kong immigration as conveniently and as fast as Mammy and Yan did. However, my ID card did not bear the three stars required to be entitled to a Home Return Permit and I needed a visa to go to Shenzhen.

At that time Hongkongers were talking about the fast development of the first Chinese Special Economic Zone, Hong Kong companies which had moved there or further north in Guangzhou province for economic reasons, and about Hongkongers working there who were keeping a Chinese mistress or a second wife.

I only returned to Shenzhen in 2004, i.e. 18 years after my first visit and could not recognise the city. Yan and I did not go to the famous Luohu commercial centre where most Hongkongers used to spend their days and money. Yan did not like that place and thought it was too crowded and had "many-mixed" (all kinds of people). Instead we went for a massage in another building nearby. Thereafter we went again a few times to have a massage there. In early 2006 we took the new underground to go to buy beads like agate and crystals to make fashion jewellery myself at home. Another time we went to Splendid China Folk Village. Today the costs of services and food have increased, but Hongkongers still go there, even though it is not as trendy as before.

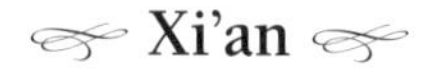

Xi'an

About two weeks after our two days in Shenzhen, we left for Xi'an via Guangzhou. We took a cross-border train from Hung Hom. From the window we could see farmers ploughing their fields with oxen. There was no tractor! When we arrived at Guangzhou railway station, just like in Shenzhen, we were assaulted by youths who wanted to change their money for our Hong Kong currency. We had planned to stay one night in Guangzhou before flying to Xi'an. When we registered at the hotel, we had to present our marriage certificate and leave our passports at the reception. But the funny thing was that we shared the same room but I had to pay more for my bed than Yan because I was holding a foreign passport. Today it is no longer the case.

The hotel was old; there was no refrigerator or TV. The only lavish item was a thermos decorated with pink peonies that we could fill up ourselves at the hot water tank in the corridor. We bought a watermelon at a street hawker but it was so hot – it must have been more than 30°C – that the fruit was warm. Once back to our hotel we put the whole piece in the sink filled with water and left it there to cool down. In the afternoon we visited the Sun Yat-sen Memorial and Yuexiu Park and the following day flew to Xi'an.

Once in Xi'an, we had to visit the famous terra cotta army of the emperor Qin Shi. My art history teacher had mentioned it and I was very curious to see with my own eyes the Eight Wonders of the World. Hawkers squatting on a large esplanade were shouting out their wares but as soon as we got off the bus, they came towards us and gathered around us hoping to sell us some souvenirs and we had to push our way through to get to the entrance.

Once in the exhibition hall, we walked slowly on an elevated path and had to extend our neck and squeeze ourselves amongst crowds of tourists – mainly locals – breathing in our neck, to get as close as possible to the security fence and have a better view. Hundreds of soldiers – some mounted on horses, the size of which depending on their roles, some standing in rows – were standing in front of me. I felt so tiny. When we left the building, we were again accosted and this time we gave in and bought miniature replicas of terracotta soldiers.

Then the worst part arrived when I looked for the toilets and saw that there was only one latrine pit. Lots of women were waiting in line. I had to relieve myself in front of a crowd. The smell was overwhelming. A few Japanese tourists were wearing surgical masks. Indeed they were very wise. Most of the touristic sites I visited had squat toilets or simple trenches. They sometimes had partitions to provide a semblance of privacy but curiously no door! There were also long queues and it was also dirty and smelled particularly dreadful. Today in large cities, there are still places where hygiene is lacking but overall the standard is higher.

There were other few unexpected things in China. For example restaurants closed very early and many dishes listed on the menu were often not available. I would have thought that the rice in China would be the best as the cereal was grown in this country and it was the staple food for Chinese, but to my surprise the grains were greyish. Today restaurants open late and the quality of service is similar to Hong Kong.

The second day we visited the Qian Ling mausoleum. I remember the sacred way with its statues of horses, warriors and mythical animals. We also visited the sarcophagus of Princess Yong Tai and other historical monuments. At every tourist place we visited where entrance fees were required, I always had to pay more than Yan. There were three rates: one for the locals, another for Overseas Chinese and a third, the most expensive, for foreigners. Today there is no differentiation and only one fare no matter what passport you are holding.

On our last day, we went by public transport to see the giant wild goose pagoda. We lined up at the bus stop behind a pregnant woman. Some men and women had rolled up their trousers and were squatting in line, while the queue was growing longer. They seemed very much at ease and I admired them since I could not stay in this position for too long. The bus was already jam-packed when it arrived and I was wondering if we would be able to get in when the people behind us started pushing and overtaking us. Where was the queue? The pregnant woman was shoved too. I was shocked. We finally managed to get in. The ticket seller forced his way through the passengers and he gave us in return two very thin paper strips. These were our tickets.

Yan and I only returned to Xi'an in 2013, or 27 years after our first trip there. The city had changed dramatically and like Shenzhen I could not recognise it. The Bell Tower with its flying eaves and the old city walls looked magnificent with its illuminations at night. I remember that in 1986 there were neither lights nor any sorts of activities at night. Today the ancient

Being pushed onto the bus in Xi'an

capital is alive after dark: shops open late in the evening and there are night markets offering a wide variety of street foods. Plazas are also very animated at night with middle-aged women performing square dancing next to Tai Chi players, each group playing its own music.

This time the hotel receptionist did not ask for our marriage certificate and we paid one single price for the room. The many bicycles of yesterday have disappeared and roads are flooded with cars. Of course the sky is not as clear as before, but when I went this year I saw that city dwellers could rent bicycles to move around the city.

Even though I already saw the terra cotta warriors in 1986, I wanted to see these spectacular ceramics again. I was surprised by the transformation of the site. It is much bigger and has more pits, includes a museum and many souvenir shops. The site is also equipped with proper toilets and hand washing facilities. The parking lot is much bigger too and filled with tourist coaches and private cars.

Chengdu

Right after visiting Xi'an, Yan and I went to Chengdu, a city well-known for its pandas but also its spicy cuisine. I really wanted to try Sichuan food.

The whole flight was scary. Before departing, water droplets from condensation were already falling from under the baggage compartments and the air-hostesses had to wipe the drips of water. Otherwise the water would have fallen on the passengers' heads!

The aircraft was small and when it encountered turbulences it was rather bumpy. During the flight, the pilot passed through the cabin to go to the restroom. When I saw he was wearing slippers I was quite nervous. Yan kept reassuring me, telling me that Chinese pilots were highly skilled and had flown fighter jets during the Korean War. Later I have taken many flights in China but these strange things never happened again.

We checked in a guesthouse and shared a room with four Hongkongers whom we had met earlier. In the city, street vendors were selling peaches and bowls of the famous Sichuan noodles (with a spicy and numbing sauce) which they carried with a shoulder pole. Young people were all dressed the same in flared jeans. Some young girls had skirts and lipstick on. Some were wearing sunglasses and kept the sticker on the lens, maybe thinking it was the brand logo. Others had kept the label on the sleeves of their suit too. Elderly men were more conservative and were wearing traditional suits and black cloth shoes. On the streets I could see many people smoking and among them a few elderly ladies. In France, it was more common to see younger women smoking than older ones.

While we were having lunch outdoor in front of a small restaurant with our new travelling companions, we saw someone falling off a bicycle. Throngs of cyclists kept flowing on the city's large avenue but none of them stopped. Just as the bus incident in Xi'an where the pregnant woman was shoved and nobody had paid attention, I was shocked by Chinese individualism. It took a while for the road traffic officer who was standing on the platform at the road intersection to descend from his podium and head to the scene. Shortly afterwards an ambulance arrived and carried the victim away.

I had a lot of spicy eggplants with pork at that lunch and I liked it a lot, but the following morning I was awakened by a pressing need. I knew I was sensitive and I was, from time to time, subject to intestinal problems. It had happened in Hong Kong and on these occasions Mammy had given me Po Chai pills and it worked well. I should have brought some with me. The little black pills looked like the small homeopathic pills my mum and I believed in, but unlike them they smelled weird. I had received cholera vaccine a month before the trip because Hong Kong had a few cases and I should not have worried. But we already bought tickets to go to the Jiuzhaigou Reserve Park near the Tibetan Plateau. How could I travel for a few hours in my condition? The bus would not stop at my whim. We would not be able to see the pandas and our tickets would not be refunded; I was sad but health came first. Later, an old lady selling vegetable steamed buns saved me from my miserable condition by telling me to eat raw garlic to treat my ailment. I ate quite a few cloves and I am sure people could smell me from miles away! Her trick worked fine. Afterwards, whenever I went for a trip I would always bring either Po Chai pills or the trumpet brand pills. Regrettably none of them taste as good as the sweet homeopathic remedy.

For three consecutive days Yan went to China Travel

Services (CTS) to try to buy two air tickets to Shenzhen, but no seats were available. The only reply he got from the employee was: "there is no ticket". Even when he explained that his wife was sick and needed to go home immediately, this did not help at all. It was quite annoying not to see any compassion or sign of hope. Today, staff members are usually friendly and helpful. During the time we waited to get tickets, we visited the city and sometimes drank tea in parks. For the modest sum of 0.5 CNY (about 1.50 HKD in 1986) we got a lidded cup and a spoonful of loose green tea leaves. We filled up our cups with hot water ourselves from a grey thermos jug. Old gentlemen in pants and grey tunics sitting next to our table were drinking tea while chatting. Drinking tea was an art in itself: the lid had to stay on the cup to trap the tea leaves in while letting only the drink out. Yan was so much more skilful than I. We could stay as long as we wanted and enjoy sipping tea in rattan chairs.

On the main street, there was a store selling souvenirs arranged on shelves in glass cabinets that only foreigners could buy. At that time local people could not buy imported good, like Coca-Cola, with local money. Their prices were fixed and had to be paid in Foreign Exchange Certificates. Yan bought me a hand-painted stone with a woman face. Street vendors offered more choices of souvenirs and at cheaper prices. We bought T-shirts with painted tigers and pandas.

Three days later we finally got our tickets to Guangzhou. I recall that the airport was not far from Chengdu city centre and our hotel. Once in Guangzhou, we took a bus to Shenzhen where we had lunch before crossing the border. When we arrived at Mammy's place, I felt very happy to have found the comfort of our room again and I suddenly felt at home.

These two trips in China had been very interesting and a real eye-opener. Xi'an and Chengdu were larger than Hong Kong and their population much larger too. China was starting to open up and the influence of Western culture started to be visible. There were already quite a few cars on the roads. However, hygiene condition and services were not good and rather backward. It was difficult to imagine that 10 years later all these places would have changed so dramatically.

I never had a chance to go back to Chengdu but I guess that like Xi'an the city has much developed and modernised.

Macau

In late August 1986, a Hong Kong friend whom we met in Paris asked me if I would be interested in being her friend's model, a sportswear designer, on a pro bono service. He was looking for a model for a commercial brochure. I was very surprised by this request as I did not fit the typical model profile – neither tall nor slim, but I accepted it on the condition that Yan came with me. It would be a fun experience that would never happen again. In addition, it gave me a chance to visit Macau. On September 7 we took the hovercraft at the Macau ferry terminal at Shun Tak Centre in Sheung Wan, and off we went!

What struck me in approaching the pier was the yellow muddy colour of the sea. Apartment buildings were not as high as in Hong Kong, and most of them were old and dilapidated. The Portuguese style apartments had verandas, closed with wrought iron grills overflowing with green plants. The avenues were lined with trees and there were a lot of small squares with people sitting on benches. The plazas' floors were covered with cobblestones or decorative mosaics which gave a Mediterranean atmosphere. The orange and pink facades of the churches and cathedrals as well as the street signs in Chinese and Portuguese on white tiles adorned with lapis blue friezes were visible signs from the colonial era.

The place chosen for the photo was the Bela Vista Hotel, one of the oldest hotels established in Macau. From the outside, this colonial style green villa built around 1870 did not appeal much to me but once I stepped in I could not help being impressed by its enormous fireplace, majestic staircase, interior balcony balustrade, and high ceilings. In spite of that, the hotel facilities were archaic and badly in need of refurbishment.

After the photography sessions, we took some time to visit Macau. On our way to see the facade of Saint Paul Cathedral, Yan showed me "Sam Ho Bakery", one of the oldest bakeries of Macau where his aunties bought cookies when he was small and spent the summer with his cousins in Macau. In the neighbouring streets vendors shouted out at us. They wanted us to taste the jerky and almond biscuits they were making in front of us. Others were attracting us with Portuguese egg tarts, another Macanese specialty. In the evening we went to the Lisboa, the famous casino of Stanley Ho[20]. We entered the main hall where the slot machines were located and played a little. I did not find it interesting to push cranks and buttons and just wait for coins to fall.

In the two days I stayed in Macau, I thought for a while I was in France, as the pace of life was more relaxed than in Hong Kong.

During the past 30 years, we went to Macau a few times. I recall that my first reflexology massage was in one of the many massage places near the hotel we were staying. We used to go to a restaurant near the Black Sand Beach which was very popular and where we played table football (foosball) while waiting for a table. We liked to eat African chicken and salted cod with scrambled eggs and fried potatoes, and drink Mateus Rosé. In the late 80s, Mateus Rosé was one of the few wines to be sold at Hong Kong supermarkets. I recall its distinctive oval and flat belly bottle. Before returning home we used to buy salted cod, olive oil in tin, and a bottle of Port.

Today some parts of Macau have become very artificial with too many casinos and hotel complexes. Luckily, the town centre remain as it was in 1986 and invokes memories in me every time I go.

Transformation in Mainland China and Macau since 1986

My next trip to China was in summer 1988 when we went to visit Kunming (Yunnan province) with Yan's eldest sister and her French friend Blandine. I did not notice many changes since my trips in Xi'an and Chengdu two years before. It was still backward and there was no attraction or anything to do at night. I remember that the buses were too crowded and we had decided to take a taxi to go to the Western Hills, but had lots of difficulties in finding one.

Then, the next time I went to China was in 1996 when Lucien and I went to Beijing to meet Yan who was teaching there for one month. We stayed for one week during which we visited the Great Wall, the Imperial Palace and other places of interests. Eight years had passed since my last visit to China. There were more shops and restaurants, and cars had almost replaced all bicycles. People were no longer wearing the same outfit and women had makeup and permed hair. The circulation of China's Foreign Exchange Certificates had stopped one year before; there was only one currency, and local people could buy imported goods. The stores next to our hotel were well-stocked but I was surprised by the price of imported goods. Even a common appliance such as a rice-cooker was as expensive as in Hong Kong. The good thing about the abolition of Foreign Exchange Currency was that nobody was bothering us to "change-money – change-money" anymore!

In 1986 I would not have guessed that the country which was so backward would have changed so much within 10 years. I recall Mammy in the late 80s bringing used clothes and food to her relatives in her hometown in Guangdong province in large red and blue stripped carry bags. At that time some merchandise was not available or too expensive for them to afford.

Then six years later, in 2002, I went to Shanghai with two colleagues from French International School. We spent three days walking around the city. Shanghai looked like Hong Kong at the end of 1980. On the Bund throngs of tourists – Chinese and non-Chinese alike – enjoyed the river scenery and the various architectural styles of the buildings lining the waterfront. Further away from this luxurious area the atmosphere was completely different: stallholders were busy washing vegetables on the pavement and craftsmen doing old trades in run-down buildings. Even further away in the former French concessions, fashionable young people were chatting in trendy coffee shops. I liked the diversity and juxtaposition of various lifestyles and atmosphere.

Afterwards Yan and I went regularly to China. We visited Hangzhou (Zhejiang), Guiyang (Guizhou), Dalian (Liaoning), Qingdao (Shandong), and a few cities in Heilongjiang province. We also went back a few times to Shanghai and Beijing. These two cities kept changing over the years and some areas are unrecognizable compared to what they looked like when I first went there.

From 2006 onwards, I went with Yan once a year

with a charitable organisation. We selected cities in the poorest provinces and gave scholarships to bright students in financial needs. We visited schools and students' families in Jiangxi, Anhui, Henan, Ningxia, and Gansu. Unlike in richer cities, the condition in the villages we went to are still backward. The same latrines I saw in 1986, with no doors, flies, and a terrible smell, are still in use.

As for Macau, the city is today more prosperous than ever before. Many casinos, shopping malls, and hotels are attracting tourists and the former Portuguese colony's laid-back atmosphere has changed into a crowded and busy place. Only the old landmarks remind me of my first trip there in 1986 and I don't enjoy going there as much as before.

Hiking and day trips

Like most of the Hong Kong population who lived in high rises in urban areas we also liked to escape from the city and went hiking. This urge to find green and spacious places was even more obvious in the first half of 2003, during the demoralising period of Severe Acute Respiratory Syndrome (SARS). Like everyone else, we avoided shopping malls and crowded places, looked for ventilated places and withdrew to the country parks. It is a strange feeling to think back of this three to four months' period. I recall that my parents sent us some surgical masks, fearing that we might be running out of stock. The Education Bureau closed all schools for one week at the end of March and then it was Easter holiday. At that time I was working at French International School and had the same holidays as the pupils and teachers. Lucien and I got a long 3-week break. Every morning I was checking anxiously the number of reported suspects, confirmed cases, and number of deaths in the newspapers. And every morning, Yan, Lucien and I went to the Joint Sports Centre of Baptist University in Kowloon Tong to run on the track. I was anxiously waiting for life to resume its course as if nothing had happened. Finally, at the end of June Hong Kong was removed from the World Health Organization's list of affected territories and I felt relieved.

Apart from designated country parks, most of the countryside was left untended. Many farmlands in the New-Territories lay fallow and neglected. Old cars and rubbishes were dumped on the road sides. Sometimes we went hiking there with our friends. Hiking was a way to discover another side of Hong Kong. We walked across many abandoned villages. Why was nobody interested in restoring those old houses? In France, this kind of old houses are particularly valued by locals as well as British and Dutch and they liked to restore the dilapidated buildings and turn them into stylish holiday homes. If Hongkongers were doing the same, more city dwellers would spend their weekends in these peaceful places.

Whenever I went hiking and lost in my dreams, I remembered how the French countryside was like. However, I was quickly brought back to reality by solo hikers listening to Cantonese opera or groups having lively conversations in Cantonese. Unlike in France, there were no walnut, sweet chestnut, or oak-trees. There were many trees but I did not know their names. There were tall trees with many layers of peeling spongy bark[21], beautiful fan-shaped leaves[22], or dangling aerial roots[23]. In old hamlets we could see banana, carambola, and papaya trees. In spring time the young leaves of tropical trees were red. On windy days the tall bamboo stalks were rubbing each other and made clicking sounds, and these small things in the nature gave me the feeling of being in Shangri-La.

I remember very well one of our first hikes with a group of sporty and experienced hikers walking up the steep shrubby trail to High Junk Peak in Clear Water Bay Country Park (in Sai Kung) in the scorching sun. It was a hard but rewarding trek as we ended with a magnificent sea view.

Later, we went with other groups of friends and I discovered many other beautiful trails. It only needed courage to get up early to enjoy a different facet of Hong Kong, far away from the crowd.

Tai O

Hong Kong had a few outlying islands and the first one I visited was Lantau, which was the largest. At that time the only way to go to Lantau was by ferry as there were no bridge and roads to link it to Kowloon yet. We had to take the ferry to Silvermine Bay. From there we took a bus to Po Lin monastery on Ngong Ping plateau and from there we walked down to Tai O, a former fishing village. The Big Buddha statue and the cable car (Ngong Ping 360°) did not exist yet.

It was a beautiful autumn day of November and we arrived in the former fishing village just in time to witness the sunset. It was kind of magical and since then I kept a special memory of this picturesque village. Tai O village is divided into two parts by a river. The main characteristic of Tai O was its houses built on stilt above water in which villagers lived on both sides of the river. The little village was sometimes called the "Venice of Hong Kong". At that time, there was no bridge spanning the narrow creek and we took a rope-drawn boat to see the stilt-houses. The woman pulling the boat was wearing a Hakka hat, a strange hat with a hole in its centre and a black veil around its edge protecting her face and neck from the sun. The river underneath the interconnected huts was very dark and the poles supporting the houses were covered with shells. Villagers were living in precarious conditions. Some homes were equipped with air-conditioners but otherwise it must have been scorching hot in summer. In 2000, a big fire almost destroyed over 90 stilt-houses. They have been rebuilt but are not in wood anymore but in tin.

On the other side of the creek, which formed an islet, there was no car and villagers were carrying heavy things in carts at the back of their bicycles. The air was infused with the pungent smell of dried seafood and salted fish. Piles of dried fish, dried shrimps, and jars of shrimp paste were displayed in front of the villagers' shops. Translucent yellowish shapes packed in plastic bags with exorbitant prices were also displayed. I discovered later that this gelatinous Chinese delicacy was called fish maw.

Nowadays we still go to Tai O. But today there is a road linking the big island to Kowloon and we usually drive from Tai Po to Tung Chung. Then we walk along the coastline all the way to the little village. Tai O is still as relaxed and laid-back as before and has not changed

Magical moment—Tai O village at sunset

Various dried seafoods in Tai O village shops

much since 1986. The only main difference is the bridges replacing the rope-drawn boats connecting the two sides of the creek. Clothes are still hung out to dry on the hut's balconies. In front of the houses, fish, duck egg yolks, kumquats, and seaweeds, depending on the season, are left to dry in the sun. Fawn and black mixed-breed dogs are lying down in the middle of the narrow streets. After our exhausting hike and before going back home we enjoy "steamed eggplants with dried silver fish" or "one-night stand fish" (fish that has been salted and left to dry for only one night) or other local dishes in our favourite restaurant, together with a beer.

Cheung Chau

Cheung Chau was the second outlying island I visited. It took us less time to go there than going to Tai O and we went to this island many times during my first years and before our son's birth.

The trip was interesting by itself and animated from the moment we stood in line to buy our ferry tickets. A crowd of holiday-makers stood as close as possible to the gate to be the first ones to embark and get a seat. And as usual, passengers would push behind us, not in an unpleasant way, but a reminder to keep moving. But Hongkongers were well-behaved and everyone moved in an orderly fashion. The ferry had two decks and first-class ticket holders sat on the upper level. Passengers sat around long tables, ate instant noodles, drank soft drinks, and played cards while listening to canto-pop music on big cassette players. In the evening once again we had to endure the same treatment when taking the ferry back to Hong Kong Island as the day trippers were anxious to get back home as earlier as possible.

On our first visit we went to the two main tourist attractions: Pak Tai Temple, and the cave of Cheung Po Tsai. The former was badly in need of a refresh. Cheung Po Tsai was a 19th century famous pirate in the Guangdong coastal area and it was said that this cave was where he hid his treasures. Frankly speaking, there was nothing to see except a cavity.

Every hour a new ferry docked, pouring each time hundreds of city dwellers onto the island, who, like us, came to enjoy a different lifestyle, fresh air and no car on their day off, so we could not escape the crowd and the noise, even when we were far away from the city. Some were going to the beach for a swim, others were cycling along the shore, and everyone was eating at all hours of the day. I would have liked to rent a bicycle but Yan was not interested in this sport and never learnt how to cycle. My dad taught me when I was small and I used to ride from my parents' home to my maternal grand-father's place, which was about 10 minutes away. I encouraged Yan many times to learn to ride but with no success.

We did not swim but stayed on the beach, sat on lounge chairs under a sun umbrella and relaxed. The air quality was better than in the city as the island had no cars and only mini-versions of fire engines could get through the island's narrow streets. In the evening we used to buy a live fish at the market and have it steamed with ginger and scallions at a nearby restaurant.

The first time I came back home from Cheung Chau, a vulgar expression came back into my head. I asked Yan what they meant. I should have guessed. Insults are the easiest phrases to remember. It is also on Cheung Chau that I learnt the word “emigration”. It was on June 5, 1989 and we were on the island with a group of friends. I could not get much of their conversation about what happened during that night. But I could see they were shocked.

We loved the laid-back atmosphere of Cheung Chau and having seafood there. However, after the birth of Lucien we seldom went there and we had seafood in a very old and traditional restaurant in Wanchai, not far away from where Mammy lived. I recall with nostalgia when Lucien helped his dad to pick up live fish for our dinner.

Integration

Jobs and Cantonese

Both working and being able to speak the local language were important issues to adapt and make my life meaningful and interesting here.

Finding a job was not easy. I did jobs that I might have never done if I had stayed in my country due to my educational background. The domain of applied arts was not something popular at that time, particularly in ceramics, and Yan did not have any connection in this field. And of course, another hindrance was my inability to speak fluent English and Cantonese at all.

During my first four years in Hong Kong I worked at the French International School. The first year I supervised pupils, then I assisted one of the kindergarten teachers in the second year, and thereafter I taught art on a part-time basis.

While working at the French International School, I discovered the "expatriates" or gweilo world. The vast majority of the French community was made of "gweilos". They were older than I was, had come to work in Hong Kong with their family and had good financial situations. They bought cheese, baguette, and other French products at a delicatessen in Central that cost about three times more than in France. I thought it was crazy. Many of them did not like going to the wet markets and did not know the names of the Chinese vegetables. They knew they would not stay in Hong Kong all their lives and did not make the effort to learn Cantonese. It was easier for me to get acquainted with locals than gweilos and developed good relationships with some of my co-workers, most of them married with Hongkongers.

I also discovered (yet superficially) a community consisting of extremely wealthy local people who were sending their children to international schools in chauffeured-cars, some living in houses on the Peak or Repulse Bay, rent of which, I was told, was outrageously high. I could not have imagined one could possibly afford it. They were members of private clubs where they could relax in a less crowded and exclusive environment. Little did I know at that time that more than two decades later I would become a member of a club.

After work I attended an English course twice a week at the British Council. I regretted of not having practised English in France, but unlike in Hong Kong, I did not have many opportunities to listen and speak that language. It was now crucial to brush up my English for my job as I needed to communicate in English with the international students. However, I also wanted to learn

Cantonese. Therefore at the same time I started to learn it by myself with the help of a manual that Yan's eldest sister gave me. I was working in a non-local environment and had few opportunities to practise, so one year later I took an extra-mural course at the University of Hong Kong. I skipped the beginner level as I had learnt the basic by myself and after having completed the intermediary and advanced level, I looked for another class but could not find any appropriate ones. There was a full time course at the Chinese University of Hong Kong, but I was working and it was also very expensive. Therefore I continued to study by myself. I recall that in the 90s I used to follow with great interest some local TV series. I also kept asking Yan many questions: he was my walking dictionary! I was eager to learn as fast as possible but realised that it was not as easy as I first thought.

Cantonese was a language difficult and frustrating to learn. There were no apps or websites to help me. Hongkongers learnt their language by the ear and nobody could tell me how to pronounce a word except by repeating it. The Hong Kong administration had never officially introduced a phonetic system transcribing the Cantonese pronunciation in Latin alphabet such as the pinyin in Modern standard Chinese. There were however several Cantonese Romanization systems but most Hongkongers were not familiar with them.

The transcription of names is not consistent. I was surprised to find Tai Po written with a "T" whereas the sound "Tai" is non-aspirated consonant and should have been written with a "D". For some other places, the sound "Tai" like in Tai Wo was properly transcribed. It was even more shocking when the name of same family members was registered differently. Yan's family name was spelled as "Cheung" whereas two of his sisters' surname was transcribed as "Chang".

Furthermore, unlike French people who assumed that foreigners could speak French, Hongkongers always thought that gweilos did not speak Cantonese. As a result, Hongkongers who were shy and afraid to use English did not speak to me, and those who spoke a little were happy to practise their English. I would have liked to tell them that I was not English and would rather practise my Cantonese but it would have only strengthened the idea that French people did not know how to speak English. Of course it was always good to practise my English with fluent speakers. However, once you started speaking Cantonese they were surprised. Even though I only spoke a few words they became curious, friendly, and talkative when I spoke in Cantonese with them.

When I first arrived in Hong Kong, it always seemed that people were shouting at each other as most sentences ended with "aa", "maa", "lak", "gua", or "la" interjections showing one's surprise or approval. I constantly heard the exclamatory particle "ah-ya!" which was similar to the French "Oh là là! ", and some words like "mat-ye" which meant "what" or "bin-douh" meaning "where". There were also lots of "ah" which was a prefix used before monosyllabic names as a term of kinship or between two people who knew each other (for example Ah-gung and Ah-po, the Chinese terms for Yan's grand-parents). The language was sprinkled with English loanwords, such as "dik-si" (taxi), "baa-si" (bus), "saam-man-ji" (sandwich). There were lots of English words that were mixed in the Cantonese sentences and lots of Cantonese colloquialisms. New slang terms were constantly created and one way to learn them was to watch TV soap operas or to stay with youngsters.

At first I did not like Cantonese because it sounded like a cacophony. With time I thought it was not that unpleasant to the ear and realised it was just as noisy and expressive as Italian. Having ½ Italian blood might have helped me to better appreciate that complicated language.

Besides not speaking Cantonese, another frustrating thing was not to be able to read Chinese. In the streets there were many hanging signs announcing businesses but I could not see what they were selling until I was in front of the shop. Hongkongers used traditional characters and the same traditional written form and the same structure as in Putonghua, but their spoken language was different. Reading aloud Cantonese or speaking or listening to Cantonese was different (for a same sentence expressing the same meaning).

In 1988 I took an evening course at the University of Hong Kong to learn how to read Chinese characters. One year later I stopped attending the course because I was pregnant, always sleepy, and did not have enough time to prepare for the dictation that the teacher was doing at the beginning of each lesson. At that time I could recognise about 1,000 characters, which was far from the 2,000 that are essential to read the newspapers.

Furthermore, one of the difficulties in reading was that names did not have capital letters. I sometimes found myself looking for the definition of characters that were part of a name. Would it have been easier if newspapers had underlined proper names? But if the Chinese, with their long history, never felt the need to do so, I guess I just needed to read more.

Then I had a chance to change job and went to work in the sales and marketing department of a local jewellery manufacturer and exporter. I was the only non-Chinese and I had lots of opportunities to practise speaking Cantonese. From time to time I had to communicate with the factory workers, for instance when I needed to chase customers' orders and push forward a special batch of rings. My colleagues taught me some colloquial expressions like "taking bus 11" which meant "to walk" due to the resemblance of the number 11 with a pair of legs. It was total immersion and I improved a lot.

I sometimes went to lunch with my co-workers in cha-chaan-teng. These places were always crowded and we had to eat in a hurry to give our seats to other customers. So later I brought my own lunch box and ate at my desk like some of my colleagues did. It was quite different from having lunch at the French International School canteen. No more full meals with starter, meat, vegetable, cheese, and fruit. And no more French baguette either! Occasionally (it was more expensive) we went to a small eatery called "The Nice Soup of the Second", "second" being a subtle way of saying "second wife" or "mistress". At that time in the early 90s, local manufacturers were moving their production to Guangzhou province as rent and labour costs were lower than in Hong Kong, and there were lots of stories of Hongkongers working in Guangzhou having love affairs and keeping a mistress in China.

I was working in a factory environment and also had to clock in at 8:30 a.m. and out at 5:30 p.m. like every other staff. I commuted by public transport. When I was living in Robinson Road (in the first two years), I took the cross-harbour bus 111 or 101 from Central to Hung Hom; then after moving to Provident Centre in North-Point, I took the ferry.

Most of my colleagues did not take their breakfast at home but bought a bowl of fried noodles or rice porridge in the street and ate it at their desks or workbenches before starting their day's work. Hot oil and soy sauce odours almost made me nauseous. I already had a cup of coffee and some toasts at home, but very soon I also bought a hot Hong Kong-style milk tea at one of the hawkers selling breakfast on Hok Yuen Street. I liked to sip my drink slowly as my colleagues were slurping their noodles.

I also had to work 5 ½ days a week and had fewer holidays than French workers had. The first year I had seven days' paid annual leave. At that time French workers were working 39 hours per week and had five weeks' paid annual leave. When I told my mum how convenient it was to be able to go shopping any day of the week, she replied that it was more important for family members to share at least one day together, i.e. Sunday, and that shoppers could make their errands on another day. You could feel the deep influence of the Catholic Church on the French culture.

My five years in this industry really helped me to understand the factory environment and the work life of local factory workers. The job was very interesting, but later I needed to travel to attend more international trade fairs. As Lucien needed more care with his homework, I decided to quit.

I did not work for about one year during which I got my driving licence, took some Putonghua lessons and did volunteer jobs at Caritas Medical Centre in Cheung Sha Wan, in Sham Shui Po District. I helped to translate to a British podiatrist what her patients were saying in Cantonese. It was not easy at all. At other times I was making photocopies in the Emergency Room. I could see accident victims rushing in on stretchers and although this was easier than the translating job, it was not pleasant at all.

My father was so happy when I told him I was learning how to drive and even happier when I successfully passed both the theory and the driving tests. He had always encouraged me to learn and advised me to do it when I was still young. I was almost 36 years old! Having a driving licence (and a car!) was very useful when one year later I went to work again at the French International School. We had just moved to Kowloon Tong and I drove every day. But I was like a mini-bus driver and only drove one route: Tat Chee Avenue to Blue Pool Road back and forth!

My new job at French International School was to assist the president of the Parents' Association. I was back to a "gweilo" environment. Most of my local former colleagues were still there and I was happy to be with them again. I had fixed hours, long holidays and therefore spent more time with my family. I also took private Cantonese lessons and enrolled in a part-time MBA course. After having worked for 10 years at the same place I started to feel bored. With an MBA under my belt and Lucien about to leave Hong Kong and study abroad, I thought I would have more time for a more demanding job and left the French International School.

I took a one-year break. However, when I looked for a job again I realised it was still hard to enter the job market, even with an MBA. Not only did I have to speak English and Cantonese, but another requirement was to be fluent in Putonghua. How could I compete with local people who could speak and write Chinese? After many months of fruitless search, I gave up. Anyhow, I was not working for financial reasons. What I feared most was people's questions about my job. I felt suddenly useless and it took me some time to accept to be a housewife. But it was a matter of culture. Yan did not mind and most Chinese men were very proud if their wife did not work. People around me were happy for me and saying that I was fortunate to be a "tai-tai", a woman who does not work and is taken care of by her husband. Was it unkind to say that? I was still young and it was a bit early to retire. In France, my parents were very anxious and would have liked me to find a job.

Volunteering

Half a year after I left French International School, I went to a charity event in a cafeteria run by an NGO where people with intellectual disabilities were trained to work in restaurants. They needed people to help during lunch time. I did not have to work for a living but I did not want to spend my time doing meaningless things. I recalled my short stint at volunteering back in 1995 when I helped to translate at Caritas Medical Centre. Helping at a cafeteria seemed more suitable for me.

A new chapter of my life started. This was also when I resumed learning Putonghua, did some beading (accessories with silver and semi-precious stones) at home, for leisure, and went more often into the kitchen (to cook!).

My volunteer job at the cafeteria was not difficult. The volunteers' responsibility was to help tidying up the tables and serving the customers. While doing these tasks, the trainees were watching the volunteers and they were following us. Luckily I was able to speak Cantonese, so it was easy but I had to learn the vocabulary specific to restaurants, like "to serve food", "the floor/eating area", etc. At first the trainees were quite shy, but after a while they became used to seeing a foreigner and did not mind speaking with me. I also taught them to say in English the names of the dishes and drinks listed on the cafeteria menu. Seeing these youngsters making great effort and working hard has encouraged me to continue helping.

About three years later the cafeteria moved to a new place but I continued to help at the new location and became even more involved. I helped there every day for two years until more volunteers had joined the volunteer team. Afterwards I went less often and started helping at another cafeteria run by another NGO. At this new eatery I helped serving the soup, toasting bread, and making drinks. I also helped at their bakery which was also employing people with intellectual disabilities. I would never have imagined when I first came to Hong Kong that 30 years later I would be helping to make one of the most traditional Chinese pastries – mooncakes – with professional bakers!

Making mooncakes for the first time at the NGO bakery

Today I still go to both cafeterias once a week and when necessary to the bakery production and training centre. I realised that although disabled persons had different needs they also had different abilities and were able to work just like "normal" people. I also found that they are more straight forward and warmer than "normal" people. I also understood the importance to integrate mentally disabled into the community. I often wonder what will happen to them if they had no job.

I also helped (for about two years) an NGO which organised arts and crafts activities in public hospitals while young patients (kids) were waiting for their doctor's appointment and parents queuing up to get medicine at the hospital pharmacy. Art was used to relieve both parents' and children's stress. If I had known when I was young about art therapy, I am sure I would have been interested to study this subject.

At the same time, during the past 10 years I have been accompanying Yan to China with another charitable organisation to help allocate scholarships to students who are bright but who cannot afford to pay the local university fees. These trips make me realise how fortunate I am and how difficult it is to live in rural areas. I have seen another facet of China that could not be perceived when I travelled to big cities like Shanghai, Shenzhen, Beijing, or Xi'an. I still continue to go each year to China with Yan to allocate students' scholarships.

All these experiences opened my eyes and I realised how education and training can change the life of youths and help them integrate into the society. I am glad to see social enterprises creating employment for people with different abilities. Volunteering work has also helped me integrate into the Hong Kong community and made myself useful. I am getting more than I am giving, helping myself more than I am helping others.

In July 2010 on a trip to Henan to allocate scholarships to students, I was asked to sign on their booklets for they had never seen a gweipo before.

Students building bridge with paper at the assessment interview in Gansu

Friendship

I don't think it was difficult to settle down as Yan was always helping me and supporting me but it was not easy to make new friends. At first I did not have my own friends and only knew Yan's friends and the Hong Kong friends we had met in France. I realised that I had to speak Cantonese if I wanted to have my own circle of friends.

The first friend I had was Lai-lai. She was a friend of Yan's and they met at CUHK when they were students. Lai-lai was always very keen to translate and teach me Cantonese expressions. Lai-lai introduced to me some of her girlfriends and on Saturday afternoons they came to our home in Chi Fu Fa Yuen to learn French. They had learnt for a few years but wanted to practise it, so I organised relaxing-type French lessons. We had many Christmas parties together at our homes. It was the days of discos and we also went dancing with Lai-lai and her friends. She loved to dance and I recall when we went between 1986 and 1990 to a nightclub called "Canton Disco" in Tsim-Sha-Tsui. The place was sprayed at regular intervals with a thick white and smelly smoke. Each time the place was sprayed, I felt like a cockroach being sprayed with pesticide. So I much preferred going to "JJ's" in the Grand Hyatt hotel in Wanchai and "Casablanca" in Aberdeen as their clientele was older and gentler. Strangely, we never went to Lan Kwai Fong in Central although there were a few discos there too. Lan Kwai Fong was not yet the hotspot into which it has developed in the 90s and is still today. I still remember our weekly hikes to support Lai-lai after her operation and what I thought was her recovery period. Sadly, she quitted us in 2006 after a long battle with cancer.

I also made other friends when I was working, and today I am still in touch with some of my former colleagues – although some of them went back to France – as well as Lai-lai's friends and Yan's old friends. I also met friends when I studied for my MBA. I was the only gweipo in the class but as I spoke Cantonese it was easy to mingle with my classmates during tutorials and when doing group projects. Today I am still in contact with some of them and we meet regularly for dinner. One of them was also my private Putonghua teacher when I resumed learning Putonghua in 2005. Later on when I did volunteer works, I met many women who, like me, gave some of their time helping NGOs. Some of them became my very good friends and we see each other quite often.

I was right to insist on learning Cantonese. It helped me to make friends and if I had not made friends, my life would have been very different.

Food in Hong Kong

Hong Kong and France are both a food paradise and for sure French and Chinese share the same passion for food. Cantonese cuisine is as varied and as sophisticated as French gastronomy. As Britain's Prince Philip once said: "If it has four legs and is not a table, has wings and is not an aeroplane, or swims and is not a submarine, the Cantonese will eat it". Sure French do not eat as many strange animals as Cantonese do and certainly no snake, but we like snails and rabbits! We also like frogs (mainly their legs), pigs' trotters, pig's ears, pig's trout, pigs' blood, and offal although they are cooked differently. We also share the same fondness for duck.

It took me some time to appreciate certain food, such as fresh bean curd, century-old eggs, and bitter gourd. The fresh tofu I saw at the supermarket in Chinatown in Paris was very bland but preserved tofu was delicious. The small white cubes of fermented tofu taste like blue cheese and I always keep a jar in my fridge to spread on toasted bread. Thousand-year-old eggs smell like the ammonia based product with which my mum used to clean sofa covers during her spring-cleaning. I still remember that strong smell; even though she had opened the windows wide to dispel the stench odour to avoid suffocation, I, locked up in my bedroom, could still hear her coughing intermittently. I could not eat bitter melon but later it became one of my preferred foods. Have my taste buds changed or has the gourd become less pungent?

In Paris I had tried tinned snake soup but later in Hong Kong I tried fresh snake soup in a restaurant. It was served with bits of deep fried dough and petals of fresh chrysanthemums – I did not know this flower was also a food! It was much tastier than the tinned soup I had in Paris.

One thing that I did not like was the presence of Mono Sodium Glutamate (MSG) in Chinese food. I did not know what it was before coming to Hong Kong, but whenever we ate outside and I felt thirsty and had an uncomfortable furry-mouth feeling, I knew that the food had been splashed with MSG. Hongkongers did not seem complaining much about it. But a few years later, more people became aware of the bad effects of this additive and restaurants started to put less or stopped adding it to their food. I was also surprised to see packs of MSG at the supermarket and MSG as a recipe ingredient (albeit ¼ teaspoon) in some Chinese cuisine recipes. Why did we have to add this food additive?

Soups

Soups held a very important place for Hongkongers and a meal was not complete without a soup. Making soups was a way for mothers to show their love to their family, particularly soups that needed to be boiled on a slow fire for a few hours.

After Yan and I had moved to our own house, Mammy used to phone us to ask us to come back "to drink soup". My mum would have never called me "to drink soup" but to "eat quenelles"[24]. Although it was not a soup, my mum would express her love by cooking the dish she knew I liked best. My maternal grand-parents were both from the Rhône-Alpes region, close to Italy and Switzerland, and my mum learnt from a young age – her mother passed away when she was 17-year-old – how to cook for her father and four siblings. Her gratin dauphinois is very good too!

I recall the first soup I made in Hong Kong. I put tomato, carrot, white turnip, and apricot kernels. I was very pleased with my Chinese style minestrone and I thought Yan would like it. But I quickly learnt not to throw anything that was in my fridge in my soups. What troubled me was that Yan could not explain to me why, but simply said that the combination of food did not match. I thought he was making a fuss about nothing. I learnt later that it was a matter of heatiness and cooling effects of food on the body, in other words of Yin and Yang. I only knew about the black and white Yin-Yang symbol representing complementary forces like darkness-light, earth-heaven, etc, but when I recalled how I felt dizzy after drinking jasmine tea, I understood the meaning. Depending on the season and the person's body constitution, different soups were prepared. Most of the soups were easy to make but what was difficult for a gweimui was to choose suitable ingredients.

Chinese also believed in the medicinal properties of plants. Like them I also believed that plants could help relieve minor disorders and treated stomach-ache or headache with herbal teas. My mum cleaned blocked tear-ducts with camomile tea compresses. Similarly, when Lucien was a baby Mammy made compresses too but with chrysanthemum – another way to use this flower! But only a few French believed in the virtues of plants and, this is why, unlike in Hong Kong where there are many herbal teas shop, in France they were non-existent and instead there were myriads of cafés. When I was small, I had a wart growing under my foot but was very afraid to have it removed. One day I read in one of my mum's books that the sap of chelidonium could burn the wart. It happened that we had a chelidonium plant in our yard. Every night I applied the plant's sap on the wart and after three weeks of application, it disappeared. It is mostly due to that experience that today I believe in traditional Chinese medicine.

Home cooking

After moving on our own in late 1986, I occasionally cooked. Yan was in charge of the cooking. He made vegetable stir-fries and soups, and sometimes "braised chicken with black mushrooms", the famous dish he made in Paris to impress me. Occasionally we enjoyed having a salad or a boeuf bourguignon (beef stew with carrots). I had a small electric oven in which I could bake leek quiche (flamiche) and bread. The supermarket in Chi Fu Fa Yuen had a limited choice of cheese, mostly "artificial" types, and not many ingredients I was familiar with. Coffee beans and wine selection were very limited. I made do with what was available and sometimes went to the delicatessen in Prince's Building to buy red wine vinegar and Dijon mustard for the salad dressing and wholemeal flour for my bread.

I liked very much steamed barbecued pork buns and decided to make some myself. I had found a recipe and already bought two bamboo steamers and was ready to try. However, when I shared with Yan my intention to make these buns, he discouraged me straight away. Nobody was making dim sum at home as it took too long to prepare and it was too difficult to achieve good results. Why wasting my time? Thus, my dim sum experience ended before having started and my two bamboo baskets became boxes for my sewing tools, old buttons, and ribbons.

Later one friend recommended me a book on Chinese vegetables written by an American woman. Always eager to try new things, a few days later I went to the Star Ferry's English language bookstore to get a copy. Her book was very useful and introduced many ways to cook Chinese vegetables, but Yan said that many recipes were not authentic and had been adapted to the taste of gweilos, but this time I did not listen to him.

When I was working I did not have time to cook, but when I stopped working I started to spend more time in the kitchen and learnt how to cook Chinese food. After all, it was more convenient to find Chinese ingredients at the wet market and local stores. Butter, cream, and milk, the most commonly used ingredients in French cooking, disappeared from my kitchen. Besides the ubiquitous choi sum and bok choy, I also bought vegetables and plants that I had never seen before such as bracken ferns shoots, pumpkin sprouts, and dragon fruit cereus flowers and later I started writing a blog on which I shared my cooking experiences (the bad ones too!).

Yum-cha

When I was in Paris Yan invited me to "yum-cha" or to "drink tea" in a Cantonese restaurant named "Hong Kong", in Saint-Michel area once a month. But there, the atmosphere and the choice of dim sum were different from those in Cantonese restaurants in Hong Kong. In Hong Kong, the restaurants were very noisy and the variety of dim sum was much larger. There was not much space between tables and patrons were sitting very close to each other. Restaurants were very big and some of them could easily accommodate over 200 customers. The decor was flashy and flamboyant. Gold signs and mythical animals such as dragons and phoenix decorated the walls. The waitresses in their cheongsam with high slits looked very sexy. The table tops could be changed according to the number of guests and the biggest tables had a rotating tray. The latter was so convenient! Each guest could pick up food easily; it was faster than passing dishes around like in France. People around the same table were using their own chopsticks to pick up food and I did not find this hygienic. Later during the Severe Acute Respiratory Syndrome (SARS) in 2003, the use of public chopsticks became widespread and it has since remained a common habit.

Hongkongers liked to go to "yum-cha" with their family. "Yum-cha" for me was a pleasant and entertaining weekend family gathering. Some patrons were reading newspapers while sipping their tea, intermittently eating dim sum. Nowadays more people are reading news on their mobile phones and many are staring at their phone screen while eating. The restaurants we went were very ordinary places bustling with noise. Yan's mum liked to drink pu-erh tea mixed with dried chrysanthemum flowers. I did not know before that dried chrysanthemums could also be used in tea. The table was overflowing with small dishes and bamboo steamers stacked on each other. The steamed beef balls were not my favourite; I found the meat too soft and I did not like the taste of cilantro inside. What a big surprise when I saw chicken feet, or "phoenix claws" as they were elegantly named, on our table! But I was very happy when I found out that chicken feet had the same texture and taste as chicken crest. When we had chicken in my family and I was small, my sister, my brother, and I took turns to eat the tiny chicken brain. When it was my turn I would also eat the chicken crest, which amused my parents. When I think of it, did I already have a predisposition to Chinese food? For sure there was more to chew on chicken feet than on chicken crest, and I will not have to wait for my turn anymore. I did not know before that Hongkongers would eat paws. Luckily they were not eating tiger or dog paws!

At that time, the most common desserts were the sweet red bean soup and the mango and sago pudding. I recall the soup my mum used to make with sago when I was small. We gave the bland starch the name of "pearls of Japan", but despite its elegant name I did not like sago. But the sweet soup made with coconut milk was very good – much better than sago cooked in chicken broth!

I liked very much the traditional restaurants where dim sums were presented on carts usually pushed by women around the restaurant floor. You just had to point to the dim sum you liked and the server would bring it to your table. It was perfect for me for I could not read the names of the dim sum displayed on the cart panels. Of course the dim sums were inside bamboo steamers and I could not see what was inside, but the attendant would lift the lids so I could look what was inside. After having selected my food, the attendant recorded my order on a small card with a stamp corresponding to the price range: small, medium, large, and special. At the bottom of the card there was also another category called "tea-tip" – which was the price per person for tea – not to be confused with bribery money! However, carts were becoming rare. When time came to pay the bill, the waiters used to shout the amount to be paid, and I found the practice very indiscreet for the person who was treating guests.

I was amazed by the dexterity, speed, and efficiency of the restaurant servers and the way they set up and cleared tables. They lent no attention to the noise made by the dishes that bumped in the basins, neither were they afraid to break them. Once a table was free, they immediately pulled off the tablecloth rolling all the waste inside. After putting another clean cover on, they would set up the tableware as if they were dealing with playing cards. The plates and bowls were like flying. The way tea was poured was equally funny. The cups were laid side-by-side and the tea was poured without bothering to stop between each cup. Tea stains dried quickly on the already well-worn tablecloth.

I never imagined that so many people would wait to get a table. In most French restaurants there was only one round of service and if they were full, you just had to go to another eatery. Here, most dim sum restaurants did not accept reservation and there were queues everywhere. Unless you came very early, you were bound to wait. Wherever we went to yum-cha with Mammy, she would go before us to get a table so we did not have to wait. When we lived in Chi Fu Fa Yuen, we used to get a number and instead of waiting at the door, we did our shopping. Sometimes we even had enough time to drop our purchases at home before being allocated a table number.

In the most popular restaurants, like the one in Chi Fu Fa Yuen, table sharing was common, but the most amazing thing was to see clients rinsing their cups, bowls, and chopsticks with boiling water before eating. I did not dare to imagine how French restaurateurs would react if their customers were doing this in France. Oh là là!

Eating with chopsticks was not a problem for me and it was handy for most of the food, but cutting long pieces of vegetables such as choi sum or big morsels of chicken with my teeth was tricky and bits of food got stuck between my teeth. On these occasions additional forks and knives would have been welcome. I was astonished to see so many people cleaning their teeth with toothpicks, covering their mouths with one hand while the other was assiduously busy. Another interesting thing was the noise people made when eating noodles. When I was small, my mum told me that it was not elegant to suck in food but here it was all right to slurp.

Just point to the dim sum—perfect for me!

Dai-pai-dong

The first dai-pai-dong that I went to was at the Bowrington Road market in Wanchai. Dai-pai-dongs were small restaurants providing simple and traditional food usually near the street markets. The service was done in a speedy manner and without any fuss. Right after being seated – on plastic stools – we were given plastic glasses and a jug of tea. This was efficient and most welcome particularly on hot and humid days. By hearing the roar of the furnace and the scraping of the ladle at the bottom of the wok, I could imagine the buzzing activity in the kitchen. The fire temperature has to be very powerful to get the special smoked flavour called "wok-hei" for which the Cantonese stir-fry technique is famous. It is difficult to do it at home.

The decor in this dai-pai-dong was simple and the walls were covered with posters with the day menu and recommended dishes. The floor was greasy and dirty. Food waste and dirty dishes were crammed into big plastic buckets not far away from our table. Despite these non-hygienic aspects, the meal was very good.

It was common in dai-pai-dong that before we finished our meal, some people were already standing behind us waiting for us to leave and take over our table. I liked to enjoy my food slowly and did not like to feel being rushed. As soon as we asked for the bill, the people waiting behind us came closer, and when we stood up they immediately took our seats. I thought these people had no manners, but later I realised that they had waited for a long time – which was very common at dai-pai-dong – and it was normal to be impatient to sit down and eat. Same as in Cantonese restaurants, I was astonished by the speed at which the service was done. In no time the table was cleared, the disposable plastic tablecloth pulled away and replaced by a new one, and clean bowls and chopsticks set. Et voilà!

I also recall another dai-pai-dong on Kowloon side where we had "claypot rice – bo zai fan" with various toppings such as minced beef and egg and mixed cured meat. It was the first time I tried Chinese sausage and I found the taste very strange as it was sweeter than the French ones and flavoured with rose wine.

Hong Kong-style milk tea

Thanks to Lai-lai, my first Hong Kong girlfriend, I discovered Hong Kong-style milk-tea. One weekend, she brought me to an old "cha-chaan-teng" or Hong Kong-style café in Sham Shui Po, on Kowloon side, to try this special tea. We sat on vinyl benches in an art-deco style surrounding. The tiled-wall was plastered with brightly coloured posters promoting afternoon tea sets and the chef recommendations. Lai-lai told me that this place served one of the best Hong Kong-style milk teas in town. I had tasted this hot drink before but had found it too bitter. However, at that eatery, the tea was very special; it was not only strong but fragrant and the unsweetened concentrated milk gave it a smooth texture. The superiority of the tea depended on the quality of the

Ceylon black tea and how it was filtered. It was said that the best teas were strained through a "used" silk stocking! Lai-lai also made me try a drink called "yuan-yang" which was a mixture of tea and coffee with unsweetened condensed milk, and Hong Kong-style French toast, another cha-chaan-teng's signature dish. The French toast was quite different from the one that my mum used to make when I was small. In France we called it "lost bread" as we used stale bread (bread from the day before). The bread was dipped in a mixture of milk and beaten eggs and then pan-fried with butter. Here, the Hong Kong style was more like a deep-fried peanut butter sandwich topped with a thick slice of butter. The butter would slowly melt on the hot sandwich and people would also pour some syrup. One toast was big enough to share between two people. Since living in Hong Kong milk-tea has become my favourite drink, although I will no longer drink it late in the

Enjoying Hong Kong-style milk tea

afternoon as I had experienced sleepless nights after drinking it.

Later when we were living in Kowloon Tong, I discovered an atypical cha-chaan-teng on Prince Edward Road West. Most of its customers were elderly men who came after walking their birds in the morning in the nearby Bird Street. The men came to take their breakfast and hung the birds' cages from a metal pole over the tables. Whenever I went near Flower Market Road to buy fresh flowers or daffodils bulbs before Lunar New Year, I liked to return to this cha-chaan-teng and indulged myself in a hot milk-tea. Later I introduced this place to my parents and some French friends. They all enjoyed the fragrant tea and the fat French toast as well as the atmosphere with the birds chirping in the background.

Crustaceans and live fish

I still remember Lau Fau Shan, a fishing village near the border with Mainland China famous for its seafood and oysters culture. It was where I discovered Hongkongers' liking for eating live seafood.

The restaurants and fishmongers were located in one same street. Shellfish and fish alike were kept in basins of water or big aquariums; they were not for display but to become our meal. I was to select one of those live fish, still swimming, and the unlucky one would later be served for my lunch and in my heart I did not feel conformable.

There were also giant molluscs looking like huge

elephant trumps. I wondered if they were put on display to be admired or if we could eat them. Most of the fish were from the grouper family. The shrimps were still moving and their prices varied according to their size and also their freshness, the less agitated the cheapest. In France we could not find live fish and shellfish (except oysters). In small towns, fish from rivers and lakes were also presented on a bed of ice. In cities far from the sea, like in Lyon where my parents lived, crabs and shrimps were even boiled and the pink crustaceans displayed on a bed of ice.

We bought our fish at one of the Lau Fau Shan fishmongers and walked to one of the restaurants nearby. The fish was making big jumps in the plastic bag, fighting for its life. We asked the restaurant to steam it with ginger and scallions, a popular Cantonese technique that keeps the fish's freshness and tender texture. I had never thought that live seafood could be so tasty and the difference of freshness with a fish kept on ice would be like night and day. Thereafter steamed fish became one of my favourite dishes.

But when it comes to freshness of food, Japanese cuisine broke all records. I will always remember when one of our friends invited us to a Japanese restaurant in Causeway Bay to celebrate our wedding and we ate lobster sashimi. I can still visualise the huge lobster eyes rolling its eyes while I was snatching bits of meat from its shell with my chopsticks. I can still see its antennae moving and its eyes looking at me. Wow! What a cruel and inhuman way of eating seafood! So far I had never had raw seafood except oysters, but at least oysters did not roll their eyes in front of me!

I still remember one particular autumn evening when we went to Lai-lai's friends to eat hairy Shanghainese crabs. Hongkongers were fond of them and liked to feast on the seasonal crustaceans. Everyone knew how to eat crabs except me. I was making a mess. The time used to remove the shell was not worth the effort. To cheer me up Lai-lai taught me to play "Black Sesame, White Sesame", a hand game similar to rock-paper-scissors. Although Lai-lai is no longer with us, I still keep fond memories of the good time spent together.

Peking duck and roast meat

French people like duck, particularly fillet of duck breast or the classic duck à l'orange, but we don't cook duck skin like the Chinese do. The first time when I had Peking duck in a restaurant, I was annoyed to see our duck being taken back to the kitchen with so much meat left on its carcass. We only had the skin! Yan immediately explained to me that this was the way Peking duck was served. Another dish, a soup, was made with the meat. The silvers of crispy skin were wrapped up in steamed pancakes with thinly sliced spring onion, cucumber julienne, and hoisin sauce. This was so elegant and tasty.

Hong Kong rotisserie was easily recognisable with the "siu-mei" or roasted meat, barbecued pork, and roast goose hung side by side in their front windows. The most intriguing stuff was the orange squids which were, in fact, not roasted but marinated in a soy-based sauce. Their deep orange colour made them look artificial.

I often missed the sight and smell of chicken rotating on spits at French markets, and the taste of aromatic herbs and spices. However, Hong Kong roast pigeon, with its crispy skin and juicy meat, was nicer than the sweet French version with peas, and as good as French roast chicken. The most exciting roast meat was suckling pig. I recall when I first tried it at my friend's wedding banquet. It was so interesting to see the waiters bringing the piglets with small red light bulbs stuck into their eye sockets to each table. It looked very ceremonious as if they were bringing a birthday or wedding cake topped with lighted candles! I could not help laughing! Talking about wedding, they ended right after the dinner (served at the table) unlike in France where we party late until the wee hours of the night. Another interesting tradition was the wedding-cheque. In France the bride and groom used a wedding gift registry service, so family and friends might contribute to the cost of tableware or wine glasses if they wished to. A recent and widespread practice was to contribute to an exotic trip for the new couple's honeymoon, or even to offer a bank-cheque. I thought that the Hong Kong practice of giving a wedding-cheque was pragmatic yet elegant as it came with a nice greeting card.

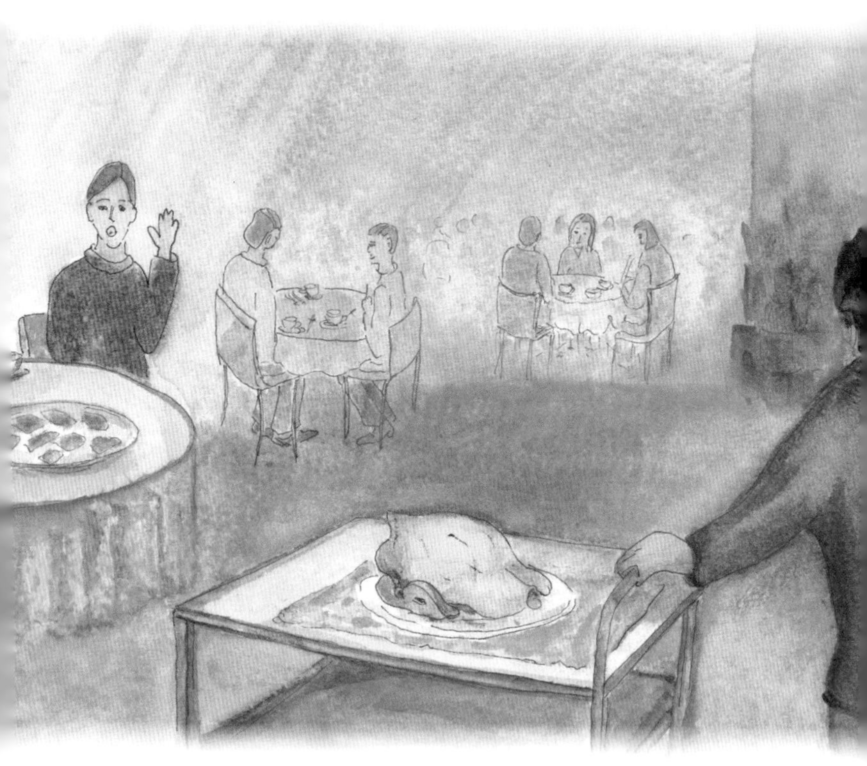

Why does the waiter take away the Peking duck with so much meat left?

Chinese festivals

Hongkongers not only celebrate Chinese festivals but also Western ones like Easter, Halloween, and Christmas. I recall one evening on my way home, I saw people dressed up as ghosts or other scary creatures in Central. Then I realised that it was October 31, or Halloween. These party-goers were going to Lan Kwai Fong to have fun. At that time Halloween was not celebrated in France. Today it is also popular, and like in Hong Kong kids dress up and knock on doors to get treats.

Lunar New Year

Lunar New Year was one of the main traditional festivals of the year. This festival was more complex than the western New Year. It was a very important period of the year when family members were getting together and the festival lasted for two weeks.

I recall my first Lunar New Year in Hong Kong in 1987. We were in mid-January and had just celebrated Christmas. I had been impressed by all the festive lights adorning the buildings, the many fir trees around town, and frenzied shopping. The year of the Tiger was going to give way to that of the Rabbit. Everyone was busy completing the many tasks to be done to welcome the New Year. Everything was new to me and I was more of an observer than a participant.

A few days before Lunar New Year, Yan told me that on New Year's Eve the stores would close earlier than usual and we would only reopen on the fourth day of the New Year, and would need to buy food and other things required for the New Year before they closed. On New Year's Eve I came home from work at about 5 p.m. Yan was already impatiently waiting for me. At that time, there was no cell phone and he could not call me to rush me to come home quickly. We hurried to Pok Fu Lam village to do our shopping but there were nothing left to buy. The sellers were busy cleaning their homes before New Year. I knew the shops would close early but I never thought they would close that early! Since my arrival in Hong Kong, I had never seen stores closed for a holiday and did not know yet the importance of Chinese New Year. Luckily we managed to find a few veggies at the supermarket, albeit not very nice, but it was better than nothing.

Homophones and decoration

Chinese language had an abundant quantity of homophones and the festival was filled with puns. Kumquat trees were displayed at the entrance of buildings as the name sounded like gold, hence symbolising prosperity;

people bought tangerines because their pronunciation sounded like luck; Mammy had posted the Chinese character "happiness" upside down on her entrance door as the pronunciation of "to arrive" and "upside down" were similar and it sounded like "happiness will come to you".

The same holiday songs were heard everywhere. Of course I could not understand the lyrics but I could feel happiness and liveliness in the music. Red and gold traditional lanterns as well as New Year greeting couplets (painted in Chinese calligraphy on a red background) were hung on each household door. TV advertisements were picturing little girls in Chinese traditional costumes dancing and singing to promote chocolates, fruit candies, and cookies, which were popular New Year gifts.

Spring-cleaning and new garments

At the end of the year, like in France, houses had to be meticulously cleaned. My mum also did a thorough cleaning before the arrival of spring. The custom of spring-cleaning originated from farmers who used to clear cellars and granaries to make space for the coming harvests. I thought there was no harm in cleaning thoroughly. Not only it was good to clean the house but the symbolic value of sweeping away bad energy and allowing good fortune to enter our home was worthy too.

It was also the time for people to replenish their wardrobe. I remembered my mum saying that my grand-parents bought new clothes and shoes for their children for New Year. However, today we can buy new clothes at any time, and with the influence of the American culture and Christmas celebrations taking over, the tradition gradually disappeared.

Flower market

On New Years' Eve, after having a family dinner, I went with Yan's sisters to Victoria Park's flower market. The park was divided into two sections: a dry section dedicated to toys, gadgets, rhyming couplets, etc. and a wet section for the flower stands. Because 1987 was the year of the rabbit, almost every item on sale had something related to this animal. The park was packed with families, elderly people, and youngsters, all doing some holiday shopping and looking for auspicious gifts and blooms. I did not buy flowers, but bought a red and golden pinwheel. Chinese believed that buying one at Lunar New Year would bring you good luck for the coming year. Although I was not superstitious, I just bought one as a souvenir. The following years we never went to the flower market on New Year's Eve but a few days before as it was too crowded. When we lived in Kowloon Tong, we no longer went to Victoria Park but to Fa Hui Park's flower market to buy gladiolus and a kumquat tree. And one month before New Year I also bought narcissus's bulbs on Flower Market Road in Prince Edward and took care of them, so their blooms filled our home with their amazing smell during New Year.

After the excitement of the festival preparations, New Year finally arrived and the city suddenly became quiet.

All the shops were closed and the streets deserted. What a peculiar sight. What had happened to the vibrant city? A red sign was posted on the shutters to indicate the day when the shops would resume business. Lunar New Year was a family business and the effervescence was now taking place in each household. On the first two days of the New Year, we went to Yan's relatives to present them our New Year wishes. I had a lot of turnip cake and year cake, two traditional treats made for this festival. On the second day of the New Year, Mammy and some relatives played mah-jong during the whole afternoon at her brother's place; they enjoyed making lots of noise when mixing the small tiles, filling the room with a festive atmosphere.

Distribution of lai sees

One of the traditions at Chinese New Year was to give red packets, also called lai sees. The distribution of lai sees reminded me when my maternal grand-father handed out a 10 franc coin as New Year present to each of his nine grand-children. In small towns and villages in France, the custom to give a monetary gift to firemen and postmen in return for a New Year calendar is still alive.

According to the custom, only new bank notes were deemed appropriate to put in the red envelopes, so people queued up at banks to get new bank notes. Chinese were very generous and the distribution of lai sees extended to a wider circle than the family. I could understand giving a lai see to the security guard of our building to thank him for his service during the year, but could not understand why we had to give to our friends who were of the same age as me or even older than me, but not married. I thought because I was not Chinese I would not have to give lai sees to our unmarried friends, but I had to.

That year, I received my first lai see on New Year's Day from Mammy. Then on the second day I received others from Yan's grand-parents, Kau-fu, and auntie no. 9. Yan and I also gave red packets that Mammy had prepared for us to Yan's cousins via his uncle and aunt.

It was not polite to open lai sees in front of the giver, so kids waited to get home to see how much money they got. On the second day, we went to watch the annual firework with Yan's friends at the Wanchai ferry pier. They were all singles and hastened to wish us a prosperous New Year, expecting to receive lai-sees from us. It was funny to see them acting like kids. It was also interesting to hear Hongkongers wishing each other to get rich because French people were reticent to talk about wealth in general and it was definitely not a French custom to talk about money. I am not sure if this was due to the deep influence of the Catholic Church.

Turnip cake and candies

At New Year Hongkongers had to eat auspicious dishes. No other dish was as lucky as Ah-gung's home-made Buddha's Delight (braised vegetables in red fermented tofu sauce) with its many auspicious-sounding ingredients.

I had heard of turnip cake a lot but only had my first

bite during the festival. I never thought it would be that soft and creamy. Before the festival, people had asked me if I had ever eaten turnip cake before and if my mother-in-law could make it. They were also curious to know if I would visit Yan's relatives to wish them a good year and distribute lai sees.

The special lacquer boxes (that Hongkongers called "complete-box') used for sweets at New Year were beautiful. Both Mammy and Kau-mou had filled in their boxes' individual compartments with chocolate coins, crystallised fruits, nuts, watermelon seeds, etc. Yan liked the milk candies with the white rabbit picture on the wrapping that reminded him of his childhood, but particularly preferred the red watermelon seeds. The seeds were dyed in red as the red colour was symbolising luck and believed to ward away evil. Yan taught me how to crack the red seeds but I could not do it well and got it stuck between my front teeth. I thought it was not worth the effort.

I will always remember when auntie no. 9 and Mammy asked me to eat candied lotus seeds. I did not know that the seeds symbolised fertility and the pronunciation sounded like "son", thus they wished Yan and I to give birth to a son soon. Yan was the only son and having a grand-son was important to keep the family name. In this regard, French families were also very traditional and keeping the family name was also important, although they would say they did not mind whether they had a boy or a girl.

Later, I would learn to make the soft turnip cake and

Ah-gung's Buddha's Delight. I would also fill up my candy box with sweets and of course lots of watermelon seeds for Yan.

Mammy asked me to have some candied lotus seeds—to bring in more sons!

Third day and lion dance

On the third day of the New Year, Yan said it was advisable not to visit family and friends. It was said that day was inauspicious for visits because arguments happened easily on the third day of the New Year. Yan could not explain to me the origin of this belief but anyhow it was better to follow the tradition and we went for a walk. About one week later, the celebrations were not yet over. When crossing the shopping centre of Chi Fu Fa Yuen, we saw a lion dance troupe performing in front of each shop. A head of lettuce tied together with a red envelope was hung above the shop entrance door. The "lion" jumped to catch the lettuce and after pretending to eat it, spat it out but kept the red envelope, which was filled with a reward for the troupe. In Chinese, the word lettuce sounds like "to make money" and therefore is meant to bring good luck and a prosperous business to the shops. The "lion" danced for a while in front of that shop then moved to another shop and performed the same ritual.

Since 1987, the festivities have not changed except that the shops reopen earlier – sometimes even as early as on the second day. And, if my daffodils were late to bloom, I did not care but today I am worried. Did I live in Hong Kong for too long and become superstitious?

The Moon Festival

The Moon Festival, also called Mid-Autumn Festival, was the first festival I experienced and I keep fond memories of the first time I celebrated it. On that evening I went to Victoria Park to admire the moon with Yan and his eldest sister. We sat on the lawn among crowds of people who, like us, came to gaze at the moon after having dinner with their family. People were eating persimmons and pomelos and of course mooncakes which symbolised family reunion. Kids were playing with lanterns and some were also burning candles in the mooncake's metal box lids. The little lights illuminating the night was a beautiful sight.

This festival reminded me of the Three Kings' Day when my family gathered to eat King Cake and "draw the kings". I recall when my sister, brother and I wished to be the lucky one and get the little porcelain baby figurine hidden inside the cake and become Queen or King of the day.

I also recall the first time I saw huge piles of mooncake boxes with pink chrysanthemums on a bright blue and gold background, in front of the stores in Wanchai. I have to admit that I was surprised by the salty taste of the moon-like egg yolk and spitted it out. However, I immediately loved the lotus paste with its soft and velvety texture that reminded me of my mum's chestnut Christmas log, stodgy yet delicious.The Moon Festival is for me the happiest and most magical of all the Chinese celebrations. It reminds me of when Lucien was small and played with paper lanterns and later with battery powered plastic lanterns representing Ultraman, rabbit, etc.

Chinese beliefs

There were many religions in Hong Kong. Mammy followed a mixture of Buddhist and Taoist practices. She paid respects to her ancestors before the family altar where a photo of Yan's dad was displayed in the apartment corridor. On festival days she burnt incense and put red-cooked meat or white sliced chicken, and rice wine in front of his photo. The food offerings were never wasted and later served on the dining table. Because Mammy believed in Buddhism on certain days she did not eat beef. She also celebrated the Hungry Ghost festival. Chinese believed that ghosts were visiting the livings during the seventh month of the lunar calendar and to appease them they were burning spiritual money or ghost money. Some of our neighbours were burning papers on the doorstep of their flat and the vestibule was very smoky. Other people were burning joss papers in braziers at the foot of their buildings.

I recall that I helped Mammy to fold bamboo papers into a shape of ingots. Some were decorated with a golden rectangle and other with a silver rectangle, representing gold bars or silver bullions respectively. I found these papers beautiful and wanted to buy some to cover plain cardboard boxes, but Yan said it was not suitable. After folding the papers we stacked them in a large plastic bag. I thought Mammy would ask me to go with her to burn them, but she did not as she was afraid that the smoke would make my eyes sting.

Joss papers were also burnt at Ching Ming and Chung Yeung festivals. On these two days, flocks of people went to visit the graves of relatives or other ancestors. Each year fire hills were caused by joss papers which had set fire to the nearby dry weeds. People also made food offerings and burnt incense. There were too many people on these two days and Yan preferred to choose another day. It was also customary on these two days to go up a mountain to avoid danger.

People were not only burning spiritual money but also paper houses, maids, cars, and even the latest mobile phones. What a strange ritual. In France we only had one special day to honour the dead. On All Saints' Day – November 1 – we also visited the graves of our ancestors and cleaned their tombstones but the sole offerings we made were flowerpots, notably chrysanthemums.

Yan's father's urn was at the Yuen Yuen Institute in Tsuen Wan. The Yuen Yuen Institute was dedicated to Buddhism, Taoism and Confucianism, the three main Chinese religions, and included temples, pavilions, prayers halls, and columbaria. The columbaria's walls were completely covered with urns from floor to ceiling – land in Hong Kong was scare and space here was precious too. I had never been to such a place before and felt very uncomfortable with thousands of black and white photographs surrounding me. Each time we went to visit Yan's dad, we would light three joss sticks and bowed three times in front of his dad's photo. Later Yan's grand-parents, Ah-gung (in 1998) and Ah-po (in 2001) also rested at the Yuen Yuen Institute. And in early 2006 Mammy also joined them there.

Another common Taoist practice was to have one's fortune told. Worshippers were shaking fortune sticks in a wooden tumbler and asking fortune tellers to tell them their future. I thought it was interesting and was curious to try, but I did not ask someone to interpret my stick as I was not superstitious. What was amusing is that the pieces of paper were the same and the mediums interpreted the same writings all year long. Later I visited Wong Tai Sin temple. Because of its popularity, the temple was very crowded with tourists and pilgrims. When crossing Wong Tai Sin MTR station, you could tell if passengers had visited the temple just by the smell of their clothes. Later in 1990, a Buddhist temple, the Chi Lin Nunnery opened in Diamond Hill, next to Wong Tai Sin temple. I much prefer Chi Lin Nunnery as it is quieter than Wong Tai Sin and there is no smoke as pilgrims cannot burn incense.

And another folk practice which I mentioned earlier was the "beating of paper figures" with shoes to have ones' enemies cursed. After watching the ritual in Wanchai (from far away), I thought it was better not to be someone's foe.

Hong Kong and China – 30 years

30 years have passed and I have changed. I recall Mammy telling me not to go to the wet market because it was too dirty and when Yan asked me to stand aside when he bought vegetables in Chi Fu Fa Yuen fearing that sellers would increase their prices because of his gweimui wife. Today I go to the wet market regularly and chit-chat with the stall holders. They are very kind and generous, and always give me lots of scallions!

I have changed but Hong Kong has changed too. The city has changed a lot in terms of urbanisation, transportation, hygiene, safety, lifestyle, and communication.

I witnessed the construction of the new airport, the longest outdoor escalator in Mid-Levels, the Hong Kong Convention and Exhibition Centre, the Hong Kong Cultural Centre, one of the biggest shopping malls – Festival Walk in Kowloon Tong and numerous buildings. Many places have changed dramatically, like Wanchai, the first area I lived in. The building where Mammy used to live on Hennessy Road was replaced by another and taller edifice and many old specialised shops were wiped out. Gentrification is taking place at the detriment of preservation. Should we not protect old buildings as part of Hong Kong's cultural heritage?

The one-screen theatres, Queen's Pier, the vehicular ferry, the rope-drawn boat in Tai O, the old double-decker buses, the guards protecting the jewellery stores and banks no longer exist. The skyline on both sides of the harbour has also changed dramatically and towers are getting taller and taller (like IFC and ICC) and the Star Ferry piers are no longer in front of City Hall. I know this is part of development and renewal but how far modernisation can go and what is its limit? I like to see new developments, but at the same time I found comforting to see the restaurant where we had our wedding dinner and the French-style café bakery where I used to go with my mother still at the same places. The harbour which has slowly been filled up with soil is getting narrower and Tsim-Sha-Tsui has never been so close to Central than today. The cost per square meter to buy an apartment has overall increased.

Hong Kong's public transportation has improved and its network expanded. There are now three cross-harbour tunnels instead of two, a bigger airport, a cruise terminal, and bridges to link the Kowloon Peninsula to Lantau Island. Today, taking the bus is easier as bus-stops have names, and it is more comfortable as there is air-conditioning. There are also more bus operators, the body of buses are covered with advertising, and audio-TV programmes are broadcast inside the vehicles. Hong Kong is also taking action to protect the environment and indoor public places and shops are no longer freezing cold.

The educative campaign on hygiene must have been effective as today it is very rare to see people spitting on the street. But at the same time as concern for hygiene has grown, the number of hawkers and dai-pai-dong has decreased and outdoor wet markets moved to indoor complexes – Wanchai Road market has moved to Queen's Road East. I am afraid Hong Kong is getting rid of its cultural assets and losing its picturesque sceneries and charm. But at the market, the butchers are still hanging meat on metal hooks in the open air. And, although quite rare, I can still see butchers smoking while cutting meat and cooks smoking in kitchen.

Work safety has also improved and even though bamboo scaffolding is still used in the construction industry, the usage of safety belts and hard hats is much more prevalent today.

The tiny Museum of Art in City Hall has moved to a new and larger building in Tsim-Sha-Tsui and there are more venues for shows such as the Hong Kong Cultural Centre and Kwai Tsing Theatre. More young people can go to universities and there are nine universities instead of two (in 1986). I also noted that they are more mixed couples and it is more common to see Chinese men married to gweimuis.

I also witnessed the change of taste of Hongkongers

and their shopping behaviour. The city is more cosmopolitan and we can find cuisine types from all over the world. People today choose to drink wine instead of brandy and take coffees and desserts at the end of their meal. As a result wine boutiques, coffee bars, and bakeries are sprouting all over the town. The once trendy Japanese department stores of the 80s have been replaced by shopping malls and some of them are very luxurious.

Fashion has also evolved and today it is not as surprising as before to see a Chinese person with auburn or blond hair. Hong Kong has also got trendier and richer than it was and today it has many brand-name and designer shops.

Landline phones are no longer prominently placed in shops, but communication is much cheaper and often free. Almost everyone has a mobile phone. I remember the giant mobile phone that one of our friends had in the late 80s. It was called "big-brother-big" and it looked very impressive. I personally got my first mobile phone in 1996, thus a much smaller and discreet version. Today with a click of the mouse or a tap on my cell phone, I can listen to French news and use an English-Chinese dictionary app. How much easier learning Chinese would have been 30 years ago if we had had today's technology!

I have also witnessed the transformation of Hong Kong from a British Colony to a Special Administrative Region and seen the bauhinia flowers replacing the Queen's head on coins, and the red, slim pillar letter boxes changed to purple and green standard boxes. Announcements in public transport which were bilingual

(Cantonese and English) became trilingual as Putonghua was added.

And last but not least, another big change is that Hongkongers are no longer shy to talk about politics.

Finding French commodities and information in Hong Kong back in 1986 would have certainly made me feel more like I were in my country but on the contrary it would not have helped me understand the Chinese culture. Learning Cantonese has been helpful in both communicating with local people and discovering Chinese culture.

China has also changed tremendously. During the past 30 years, China has developed at a very fast pace and caught up with Hong Kong in terms of urbanisation, transportation, services, and communication. The Shenzhen and Xi'an which I visited 30 years ago are quite different from the cities they used to be in 1986.

The rice fields in Shenzhen have been replaced by high-rise buildings, hotels and shopping malls. The streets which used to be full of bicycles are now crowded with private cars and there are traffic jams and more pollution. Who could have foreseen all these changes? I can't recognise the Shenzhen I saw the first time in 1986.

Since 1995 there is only one currency and Foreign Exchange Certificates that used to entitle only foreigners to buy imported goods have stopped to exist. Nowadays you can buy Coca Cola everywhere and the price of a hotel room is the same for both Chinese and non-Chinese. The many shopping malls are full of various commodities and luxurious goods, which is a huge change from the old days when local stores offered a limited choice. There are things to do at night and unlike in the old days when lunch and dinner were served at a certain time, you can find something to eat at any time of the day and night. The quality of service in restaurants is now comparable to that in Hong Kong. People do not dress in Mao jackets anymore but wear fashionable clothes, the same as we can see in Hong Kong. Shenzhen and Xi'an have also launched a bicycle rental service to encourage their inhabitants to use bicycles to move around the city. Square dancing is now a popular exercise, but Tai Chi has still a lot of followers.

30 years ago, Mammy used to bring old clothes to her relatives in China. Today it is not necessary as the population is much wealthier than before. I also recall in the 90s when it was trendy to go shopping in Shenzhen. Today the Hongkongers go less often to Shenzhen and instead we see huge numbers of Mainland Chinese coming to do their shopping in Hong Kong. But despite this apparent wealth in all the major cities, I have seen schools in villages in poor areas like Gansu and Henan provinces which were badly in need of modernisation and still backward in terms of hygiene.

In comparison, during all these years, I went back regularly to my hometown in France. Although many new residential developments and private houses have been built, the overall landscape did not change that much as compared to the changes I saw in Hong Kong and China. Of course my hometown is small. The number of working hours has been reduced to 35 hours per week. French economy is not doing well and more French people are looking for jobs abroad. Another reason is the high income tax rate. As a result the French community in Hong Kong has increased tremendously from 2,000 in 1986 to over 16,000 today. But, unlike before, most of the French coming here are no longer employed on "expatriate's term" but are mostly young entrepreneurs.

Conclusion (without ending)

My past 30 years have been full of surprises. Besides learning about Chinese culture, I also did things I had never imagined I would do. I had done jobs that I never thought I would do. I worked both for schools and private companies, and experienced French and Chinese work culture. I got an MBA, discovered volunteering work and met great people. I learnt Cantonese and Putonghua. I got a chance to meet bright students in China and work with people with intellectual disabilities. These experiences have allowed me to integrate into the society and at the same time to contribute to the Hong Kong community. I have lived in seven different districts, each time moving further away from the city, and I discovered new areas. I also experienced the bird flu crisis and SARS. And last but not least, if the most challenging and beautiful experience was to be a mother, the most precious gift of my life has been my son Lucien.

Hong Kong might not look the same as before,

but intangible things like the celebrations of festivals and the underlining superstition in the daily lives of Hongkongers have not changed. I have aged but I still love to eat steamed fish and drink a cup of Hong Kong-style milk-tea, and from time to time go to Tai O to enjoy the village's charms and its local dishes. And the most important thing is that my love for Yan is still the same if not stronger and our son is a grown-up and independent young man who keeps in touch with Yan and I and shows his love for us.

Notes

1 Gweimui is the slang term for a young Caucasian girl (gwai2-mui2 鬼妹 – lit.: ghost-younger sister).
2 Gweipo is the slang term for a Caucasian woman (gwai2-po4 鬼婆 – lit.: ghost-older woman). Gweilo 鬼佬 – is the slang term for Caucasian and refers to foreigners in general and is non-derogatory.
3 There is an American cooking series on the US public television, "Yan can cook" (http://www.yancancook.com/)
4 Consisting of dipping pieces of meat into hot oil.
5 Consisting of dipping bread into melted cheese.
6 A very old Citroën model.
7 Michael Jackson – Thriller.
8 A commuter rail service (serving Paris and its suburbs).
9 The Million – published by Hachette – an Encyclopedia of all countries.
10 Lydia Shum – Fei-fei (肥肥).
11 The Million (see note 7).
12 The current one designed by Foster.
13 Designed by I. M. Pei & Partners.
14 The Avenue of Stars was officially opened in 2004.
15 1 HKD was equivalent to about 0.70 FRF (in 1985). 1USD = 7.8 HKD.
16 Hong Kong Dollars (HKD) – 1 USD is pegged at 7.78 HKD.
17 The murder of Braemar Hill (寶馬山) on April 20, 1985.
18 Chocolate sweets with silver or gold fringe wrappings originating from Lyon.
19 Red envelope filled with money.
20 Stanley Ho Hung Sun is a Hong Kong and Macau tycoon. He is nicknamed "The King of gambling".
21 Paper-bark trees.
22 Ginkgo trees.
23 Ficus Microcarpa or Chinese banyans (細葉榕).
24 Light dumplings and one of the specialties from Lyon.

Acknowledgments

I thank my parents who let me fly to the other side of the world 30 years ago and supported my decision to marry Yan, a Chinese man whom they knew little about.

I thank my mother-in-law who accepted me as her own daughter and took great care of her grand-son, as well as my sisters-in-law, Emily, Brigit, Eva, Fanny, and Alethia, who treat me as their sibling.

I am grateful to my friends for encouraging me to write and share my story with you. I am sure Lai-lai would have done the same, had she been with us today.

I thank Mr. Mao Yong-bo and Ms. Janice P.C. Yip of Commercial Press for their guidance in my writing of this book. Their clever suggestion of illustrating some scenes with sketches has allowed me to revisit fond memories through my drawing skills acquired decades ago.

My thanks also go to my former Mandarin teacher, Ms. Tang Xiao-sha, who skilfully translated my story, and Ms. Doreen Cheng and Mr. C.K. Woo who helped me in the preparation of the manuscript.

My deepest thanks go to my husband for his

continuous patience, care, and encouragement to learn Chinese and discover the real and local side of Hong Kong. Without him, I could not have adapted to living in Hong Kong, a place that I now call home. Without him, this book could not have been possible.